Layman's Bible Book Commentary
1, 2, & 3 John, Jude, Revelation

LAYMAN'S BIBLE BOOK COMMENTARY

1, 2, & 3 JOHN, JUDE, REVELATION

VOLUME 24

Fred D. Howard

BROADMAN PRESS
Nashville, Tennessee

4211-94

ISBN: 0-8054-1194-1

Dewey Decimal Classification: 228
Subject Headings: BIBLE. N. T. JOHN (EPISTLES) / / BIBLE. N. T. JUDE / /
BIBLE. N. T. REVELATION

Library of Congress Catalog Card Number: 80-66807

Printed in the United States of America

Foreword

The *Layman's Bible Book Commentary* in twenty-four volumes was planned as a practical exposition of the whole Bible for lay readers and students. It is based on the conviction that the Bible speaks to every generation of believers but needs occasional reinterpretation in the light of changing language and modern experience. Following the guidance of God's Spirit, the believer finds in it the authoritative word for faith and life.

To meet the needs of lay readers, the *Commentary* is written in a popular style, and each Bible book is clearly outlined to reveal its major emphases. Although the writers are competent scholars and reverent interpreters, they have avoided critical problems and the use of original languages except where they were essential for explaining the text. They recognize the variety of literary forms in the Bible, but they have not followed documentary trails or become preoccupied with literary concerns. Their primary purpose was to show what each Bible book meant for its time and what it says to our own generation.

The Revised Standard Version of the Bible is the basic text of the *Commentary*, but writers were free to use other translations to clarify an occasional passage or sharpen its effect. To provide as much interpretation as possible in such concise books, the Bible text was not printed along with the comment.

Of the twenty-four volumes of the *Commentary*, fourteen deal with Old Testament books and ten with those in the New Testament. The volumes range in pages from 140 to 168. Four major books in the Old Testament and five in the New are treated in one volume each. Others appear in various combinations. Although the allotted space varies, each Bible book is treated as a whole to reveal its basic message with some passages getting special attention. Whatever plan of Bible study the reader may follow, this *Commentary* will be a valuable companion.

Despite the best-seller reputation of the Bible, the average survey of Bible knowledge reveals a good deal of ignorance about it and its primary meaning. Many adult church members seem to think that its study is intended for children and preachers. But some of the newer translations have been making the Bible more readable for all ages. Bible study has branched out from Sunday into other days of the week, and into neighborhoods rather than just in churches. This *Commentary* wants to meet the growing need for insight into all that the Bible has to say about God and his world and about Christ and his fellowship.

BROADMAN PRESS

Contents

THE LETTERS OF JOHN

2 JOHN

3 JOHN

JUDE

REVELATION

1, 2, 3 JOHN

Introduction

The Johannine Epistles traditionally have been classified among the General Epistles (including James, 1 and 2 Peter, Jude, and, rightfully, Hebrews). In contrast to the Pauline Epistles, the General Epistles were not addressed to a specific person or church. However, 3 John was written to a particular Christian named Gaius.

Authorship

According to a rather strong Christian tradition, the apostle John wrote these three letters, together with the Gospel and Revelation. Even from early times, however, the case for Johannine authorship of 1 John has been stronger than that for the Second and Third Epistles. The chief reason is that the writer of 2 and 3 John referred to himself as "The elder." Although there is biblical evidence that apostles sometimes were called elders (1 Pet. 5:1), certain of the early church fathers made a distinction between John the Apostle and John the Elder. Since the distinction was based on meager and doubtful evidence, there is no compelling reason to reject the traditional view that the apostle John wrote all three letters.

Nature and Purpose

First John is more in the form of a homily than a letter. It has no greeting, no mention of names, and no salutation. Yet the tone is very personal and clearly implies that the writer knew his readers intimately. Even a casual reading of 1 John reminds one of the similarity between it and the Gospel. Expressions such as *word, truth, light, darkness,* and *love* are abundant in both writings. Both in the Greek originals and in the English translations, the simple style that characterizes the Gospel also carries over into the Epistle. Despite the simplicity, however, the content is profound.

In contrast to the evangelistic purpose of the Gospel (John 20:31), the stated purpose of 1 John is to assure Christians of their salvation

(5:13). Another clear purpose of 1 John is to warn the Christian community about false teachers, presumably Gnostics, who denied the reality of the incarnation. John also refuted the Gnostics in the prologue to his Gospel and in 2 John. Additionally, we find in 1 John the author's desire for his readers to attain spiritual maturity in both attitude and action.

As already indicated, the purpose of 2 John was to refute gnostic teaching and to repudiate those who spread it. Both 2 and 3 John deal with traveling teachers. Second John is concerned with false teachers, whereas 3 John refers to bearers of the truth who had been rejected by a dictatorial leader of the church named Diotrephes.

Destination and Date

Overwhelming evidence indicates that the apostle John spent his last years in and around Ephesus, which was located in the Roman province of Asia. Apparently he remained in exile on the island of Patmos (Rev. 1:9) until the death of the emperor Domitian. Although we do not have exact knowledge, we may reasonably assume that all three epistles were addressed to churches in the Asian province. Despite the impossibility of determining the sequence of the writings, we have sufficient evidence to conclude that all were written in the approximate time span of AD 90-95.

1 JOHN

Prologue:
Eternal Life Revealed in Christ
1:1-4

The similarity between the introduction to this epistle and the Gospel of John is quite obvious. Many readers interpret the similarity to indicate common authorship. Assuming that the apostle John wrote both, we next must decide which he wrote first, the Gospel or the Epistle. For example, the prologue of the Gospel (1:1-18) may very well be a development and a refinement of the prologue to the Epistle. On the other hand, the less personal description of the "word" in 1 John may mean that the author assumed his readers' knowledge of his Gospel's prologue.

Five central ideas stand out in the epistle's prologue: (1) the eternal preexistence of the Word; (2) the historical manifestation of the Word; (3) the proclamation of the Word; (4) the purpose of Christian fellowship; and (5) the purpose of fulfilled joy. Also, in common with the Gospel, the terms *word* and *life* are prominent (v. 1).

Unquestionably, John used the expression "the beginning" to refer to eternity, not to historical time. Thus, Christ is the eternal Word, coexistent with the Heavenly Father. Despite our inability to comprehend the nature of the divine Trinity, the Scriptures teach that the one God somehow has manifested himself in threeness as Father, Son, and Holy Spirit (Matt. 28:19).

In his use of the verbs "have heard," "have seen," "have looked upon," and "touched," John stressed the reality of the historical manifestation of the Word. Because certain professed Christians, usually identified as Gnostics, denied the reality of the incarnation, John attempted to refute such a heretical view by appealing to his firsthand experience with the historical Jesus. The Gnostics mistakenly believed that matter was evil and denied that God became flesh in the person of Jesus. In so doing, they tried to separate the Christ of faith from the Christ of history.

John appealed to the senses of hearing, sight, and touch to prove

13

that the body of Jesus was not a phantom but an actual body. Even the resurrected body of Christ was tangible and real. Perhaps John recalled Thomas's doubt and demand to feel Jesus' body (John 20:25). Certainly John must have remembered Jesus' challenge when he said, "handle me, and see; for a spirit has not flesh and bones as you see that I have" (Luke 24:39). The Greek word for "touched" in verse 1 is translated "handle" in Luke 24:39. It means to grope for something, not merely to "touch." The words denoting sight in verse 1 are significantly different. The first means to see, and the second means to gaze upon, as in a theater.

By "word of life," did John mean the proclaimed word, that is, the gospel, or the incarnate Word, Jesus Christ? The expression may mean the word which itself is life or the word which produces life. Although the gospel "is the power of God for salvation" (Rom. 1:16), the "word" here, as in John's Gospel, seems to refer to Christ. Eternal life is the result of knowing "the only true God, and Jesus Christ" (John 17:3).

God always takes the initiative in salvation. This declaration is true both in terms of God's overall redemptive act and also his individual acts of salvation. Christ who is life incarnate, and who also gives life, "was made manifest," that is, openly revealed to mankind (v. 2). In addition, Christ both is and gives "eternal life." Although the word translated "eternal" means agelong, in biblical usage it denotes quality as well as quantity. From the viewpoint of quantity, it lasts forever. Yet so does eternal death—which means eternal separation from God, not cessation of existence. Qualitatively, eternal life means everlasting fellowship with God and with all others who know God in the forgiveness of sin.

Because eternal life is so wonderful, it carries with it an imperative to be shared with others. John and his Christian contemporaries felt an inner compulsion to share the gospel (1 Cor. 9:16). The word "testify" means to bear witness. John was an eyewitness of God incarnate in the person of Jesus. The experience was so thrilling and liberating that he desired to tell others about it. Thus, John was a living martyr (witness) in the true sense of the word.

John also was a messenger. The word rendered "proclaim" means to report or to announce. The root word is the basis for angel (messenger). Like the herald angel (Luke 2:9-12), John had good news to be proclaimed. In fact, he was so excited that he repeated himself (v. 3). Perhaps John repeated his words to emphasize his refutation of the Gnostic heretics.

One stated purpose of John's proclamation is "so that you may have fellowship with us" (v. 3). We cannot be certain whether "us" should be taken in the editorial sense or whether it refers to the joint apostolic witness to the incarnate Christ. The word translated "fellowship" can also mean communion, sharing, and participation. It means a partnership in a common experience, enterprise, or purpose. The basis of Christian fellowship is the shared experience of knowing Jesus Christ as Savior and Lord. Such fellowship has both vertical and horizontal dimensions. Vertically, fellowship is "with the Father and with his Son Jesus Christ." Horizontally, it includes all others who share in such a faith relationship.

John expressed a second purpose for writing, "that our joy may be complete" (v. 4). Although "your joy" seems more natural than "our joy" in the context, manuscript evidence is divided, with stronger support for "our joy." The difference, however, is minor since "our joy" is wide enough to include "your joy." The end result or fruit of fellowship is joy. God's children are to be joyful, and something is wrong when they are not. Like peace, real joy does not depend on external circumstances. Thus, Paul rejoiced even while in prison and encouraged his readers to "Rejoice in the Lord always" (Phil. 4:4).

Living in the Light
1:5 to 2:17

Light Versus Darkness (1:5-10)

The author further identified his "message" by affirming "that God is light and in him is no darkness at all" (v. 5). Throughout the Bible, God is characterized as light. The same is true of the Essene literature known as the Dead Sea Scrolls. The prologue of John's Gospel makes many references to light. For example, Jesus is the "true light" (John 1:9). Later Jesus identified himself as "the light of the world" (John 8:1). Jesus also taught that "men loved darkness rather than light, because their deeds were evil" (John 3:19).

Just as God is characterized as light, sin is characterized as darkness. Since light and darkness are mutually exclusive, there can be no darkness in God. Because God is holy (Lev. 11:44), he is the exact opposite of sin and cannot "behold evil" (Hab. 1:13). Although God loves sinners, he hates sin and is eternally opposed to it. Since God is holy, he demands holiness in his children (Lev. 11:44). Consequently, the goal for the believer is nothing less than the moral perfection of God (Matt. 5:48) or of Christ (Eph. 4:13).

The gnostic heresy took two opposite views toward the body and sin. One group held that since the body was essentially evil, sins of the flesh did not affect a person spiritually. Accordingly, they succumbed to temptations and defended their actions by claiming that Christian freedom liberated them from moral restraints. Their attitude and actions labeled them as libertines or antinomians (those against moral law). The other group took the ascetic approach to their bodies. Instead of giving in to the flesh, they denied it. Later historical expressions of this tendency were the monastic movement and particularly the Flagellants and Penitentes who abused their bodies in a misdirected effort to please God. Oddly, both groups, since they viewed salvation as the result of knowledge (*gnosis*) instead of faith, believed in the attainment of sinless perfection. However, this tendency was more characteristic of the ascetic group.

The expression "If we say" is the author's way of pointing out the fallacy of the antinomian view (v. 6). Thus, people who claim to "have fellowship with him" and yet "walk in darkness" are liars. Dealing with the same problem, Paul asked, "Or what fellowship has light with darkness?" (2 Cor. 6:14). The additional statement, "do not live according to the truth," shows clearly that faith cannot be divorced from practice. People who claim to know the truth live a lie if they do not practice the truth. Christians are to "be doers of the word, and not hearers only" (Jas. 1:22). God's imperative has always been to trust and obey, and always in that order.

In contrast to the libertine attitude and life-style, "if we walk in the light, as he is in the light, we have fellowship with one another, and the blood of Jesus his Son cleanses us from all sin" (v. 7). The meaning of the conditional clause is that our daily lives are to correspond with the ethical values that Jesus both personified and taught. Even though we shall occasionally stumble, we are never to lower the divine standard. The fruit of such a spiritual pilgrimage is fellowship both with God (and Christ) as well as with one another. Being children of God automatically makes us spiritual brothers and sisters, and because we are his children we are increasingly to put on his character.

While we cannot know precisely how "the blood of Jesus his Son cleanses us from all sin," we have the assurance that it does. According to biblical usage, blood is symbolic of life (Lev. 17:11-14). The blood or the death of Christ refers to his life laid down as a self-sacrifice for our sins. Paul set forth this truth when he wrote "justified by his blood," "reconciled . . . by the death of his Son," and "saved by his life" (Rom. 5:9-10). In Revelation 1:5 we read that Christ "freed [loosed] us from our sins by his blood" or "washed us from our sins in his own blood" (KJV). Regardless of which reading is the original, Christ's death for our sins, along with his resurrection, is the heart of the gospel (1 Cor. 15:3-4).

Verse 8 likely was aimed in particular at the ascetic group: "If we say we have no sin, we deceive ourselves, and the truth is not in us." Although some interpreters take "sin" here to mean the Adamic nature of humanity's basic estrangement from God, such an interpretation is uncertain. The same interpreters believe that verse 10 refers to acts of sin. However, whether John meant sinners by nature or practice (or both), those who deny their involvement in sin deceive themselves. Occasionally they may even deceive others, but they never deceive God. In addition, such people are liars, because God has declared that all are sinners (Rom. 3:23). Besides, if people were not sinners, the incarnation, death, and resurrection of Christ would have been utterly unnecessary (Matt. 9:13).

Confession, not denial, is the divinely ordained answer to our sin problem (v. 9). We must come under God's judgment before we come under his grace. Self-righteousness was the besetting sin of the Pharisees and the Jews as a whole (Rom. 10:3). The verb "confess" comes from two words, *like* or *similar* and *to say.* Consequently, to confess sin is to say the same thing that God has declared about it. The character of God is such that "he is faithful and just, and will forgive our sins and cleanse us from all unrighteousness." People may sometimes be liars, but God never is (Rom. 3:4).

The basic idea of "forgive" is to remit (as a debt) or to send away (Ps. 103:12). The scapegoat on the Day of Atonement was symbolic of God's forgiveness (Lev. 16:7-10). Divine forgiveness means that

God no longer holds our sins against us. God also cleanses us "from all unrighteousness." Although forgiveness and cleansing from sin in one sense are a once-for-all experience, the language here shows that forgiveness and cleansing are continual. The reason, of course, is that Christians continue to sin, not as a permanent life-style, but they occasionally yield to temptation or otherwise fail to live according to God's expectations.

Unless we interpret verse 10 to refer only to acts of sin, it largely repeats the substance of verse 8. One distinct difference, however, is the verb tenses. Whereas the present tense appears in verse 8, the perfect tense appears in verse 10. Thus, no one can truthfully say that he is presently sinless (v. 8); neither can he truthfully say that he has never sinned (v. 10). In addition, some see in the passage a heightening order of sinful rebellion: (1) affirming a lie; (2) deceiving oneself; and (3) making God a liar. In reality, of course, no one can actually make God a liar. Yet to deny one's sinfulness in effect makes God a liar and proves the absence of God's word in such a person. Self-righteousness is the worst form of blasphemy.

Christ Our Advocate (2:1-6)

Jesus set the moral perfection of God as the Christian ideal (Matt. 5:48). John stressed his epistle's purpose in the words, "so that you may not sin," that is, commit acts of sin (v. 1a). The expression, "little children," refers not to age but to John's affection for his readers. Despite the ideal of sinlessness, John conceded that Christians never reach that ideal on earth by adding, "but if anyone does sin, we have an advocate with the Father, Jesus Christ the righteous" (v. 1b). Again John used a verb tense that indicates acts of sin, not a life-style of sin.

The word translated "advocate" means one called alongside and may be rendered comforter, helper, or aide. The same term occurs several times in John's Gospel to designate the Holy Spirit and appears in English as Counselor (Comforter, KJV). Jesus identified himself with the Holy Spirit or Counselor (John 14:16-18).

As our "advocate," Jesus is the "one mediator between God and men" (1 Tim. 2:5). Somewhat like a defense attorney, but more like a priest, Christ "is able for all time to save those who draw near to

God through him, since he always lives to make intercession for them" (Heb. 7:25). As John put it, Christ "is the expiation for our sins, and not for ours only but also for the sins of the whole world" (v. 2).

The word translated "expiation" also may be rendered "propitiation," which in pagan religions involved appeasement of the offended god. The root word is also the basis for the term *mercy seat*. Although some use expiation and propitiation synonymously, others insist that expiation refers to a sacrifice which cancels sin but does not involve appeasement. Despite differences of opinion, we must remember that God took the initiative in salvation and somehow became flesh in the person of Jesus Christ who through his death and resurrection accomplished salvation for all who trust him as Savior and Lord. Paul expressed this truth when he wrote that "In Christ God was reconciling the world to himself" (2 Cor. 5:19). As verse 2 clearly states, Christ died "for the sins of the whole world," not merely for the sins of Christians or the elect (chosen). The only thing that prevents everyone or anyone from being saved is unbelief.

Against the libertine Gnostics who claimed that sin in a Christian's life did not matter, John asserted that obedience is the mark of a true Christian. In fact, "we may be sure that we know him, if we keep his commandments" (v. 3), which is the equivalent of keeping "his word" (v. 5). On the contrary, "He who says 'I know him' but disobeys his commandments is a liar, and the truth is not in him" (v. 4). Although the Ten Commandments are still valid for believers, John no doubt referred to the commandments of Christ. Perhaps Jesus' primary commandments are the command to love (John 13:35) and the command to bear witness to him (Matt. 28:19-20; Mark 16:15; Luke 24:47; John 20:21; Acts 1:8). According to John, "love for God is perfected" or brought to its intended goal by obedience (v. 5). Christians are "to walk" (conduct their moral lives) as Christ "walked" (v. 6).

Love, the Old-New Commandment (2:7-11)

In what sense is the commandment to love both old and new? It is at least as old as the Mosaic law. For example, we read in Leviticus 19:18 that "you shall love your neighbor as yourself." Then we read in Deuteronomy 6:5, "and you shall love the Lord your God with all your heart, and with all your soul, and with all your might." Jesus said, "On these two commandments depend all the law and the prophets" (Matt. 22:40). The words, "which you had from the beginning," (v. 7) probably mean that the command to love was the first precept learned by Christians.

By "new commandment," John likely referred to Jesus' statement: "A new commandment I give to you, that you love one another; even as I have loved you, that you also love one another" (John 13:34). Jesus himself gave new dimension to love. In his own person, he was the greatest manifestation of divine love, particularly as demonstrated by his sacrificial death for sinners. The new commandment to love was "true [real] in him [Christ] and in you" (v. 8). Both Jesus and his followers were personal examples of divine love. The "true light" is Jesus (John 1:9) who dispels spiritual darkness (John 1:5).

As used by John, "light" and "love," like "darkness" and "hate," are respectively interchangeable. Thus, one who claims to be "in the light," that is, a true disciple of Christ, "and hates his brother is in the darkness still" (v. 9). Verses 10 and 11 repeat this truth and add that the one who loves does not offend others, while the one who "hates his brother" walks aimlessly in the darkness "because the darkness [hate] has blinded his eyes" (v. 11). Therefore, hate is self-destructive.

Obedience, the Overcoming Life (2:12-17)

Verses 12-14 seem to be a poem modeled somewhat after Hebrew parallelism. The writer addressed "little children," "fathers," and "young men," in that order, twice. Each time he said the same thing to the fathers, but he varied his statements to the little children and young men. Two other differences stand out. In the first stanza, John used the present tense of the verb all three times. The usual translation of the present tense is "I am writing" in contrast to "I wrote." "I write" is preferable to "I wrote."

The second difference is in the terms for children. In verse 12 the word means "little children" from the standpoint of birth and relationship to parents. However, the word "children" in verse 13 means "little children" in terms of age and is the root word for "pediatrics." John possibly used the words interchangeably here since he used the first (2:1) and the second (2:18) as terms of endearment for all Christians.

Some Bible students do not believe that John addressed specific age groups because of the fact that he mentions fathers before young men. In addition, the words applied to each age group do not particularly suit that age group. Because of these and other reasons many interpreters have concluded that John meant three stages of spiritual development. A further refinement is the idea that a Christian may be all three at the same time. For example, despite the disparagement of spiritual bottle babies elsewhere (1 Cor. 3:1-2; Heb. 5:13), Peter advised his readers, "Like newborn babes, long for the pure spiritual milk, that you may grow up to salvation" (1 Pet. 2:2).

Assuming the view of spiritual progress, we note that forgiveness is both an initial and a basic experience for all Christians (v. 12). Although even the very young in Christ know God or Christ (v. 13), the more mature believers designated as "fathers" have a more intimate knowledge of God. Perhaps because youth are characterized by strength, those called "young men" had overcome Satan in their lives (vv. 13-14), particularly in the matter of temptation (vv. 15-17). The fact that the young men had the "word of God" abiding in them suggests that they appealed to God's Word to overcome Satan's temptations just as Jesus had done (Matt. 4:4,7,10).

The command, "Do not love the world" (v. 15), does not mean the world of people as in John 3:16. Rather, it refers to the world as in opposition to God, to the world system of selfishness and sin as compared to the self-giving and righteous nature of God. The added words, "or the things in the world," include materialism just as Jesus said, "You cannot serve God and mammon" (Matt. 6:24).

The main thrust of verse 16 is a prohibition of sensuality or sins of the flesh. Like Paul, John used "flesh" in an ethical sense to refer to base desires. Although the word translated "lust" may mean desire in a good sense, here it clearly means lust or unbridled desire. In the expression, "pride of life," the word translated "life" is the basis of our word *biology* and designates people in their humanity. "Pride of life" may mean pride in one's material possessions and denotes a boastful attitude. Worldly people prove both by their attitudes and actions that they do not know God.

In contrast to the transient nature of the world and its lust, "he who does the will of God abides for ever" (v. 17). The expression, "the world passes away," however, does not refer to the extinction of the earth. Rather, the earth awaits purification and renewal (Rom. 8:19-23).

The Last Hour
2:18-29

Many Antichrists (2:18-23)

John, as well as New Testament writers in general, wrote as if Jesus might return in his own lifetime. Perhaps such anticipation was more of a hope than a prediction. Thus, the term "last hour" expresses joyful longing for Christ's soon return. Lest we accuse John of being mistaken, we should remember that Peter wrote "that with the Lord one day is as a thousand years, and a thousand years as one day" (2 Pet. 3:8).

The term "antichrist" appears scripturally only here, in 4:3, and in 2 John 7. Literally the term means "against Christ," but it also can mean one who substitutes himself for Christ. Jesus had warned, "For many will come in my name, saying, 'I am the Christ,' and they will lead many astray" (Matt. 24:5). Jesus also said, "For false Christs and false prophets will arise" (Matt. 24:24). For example, in the Jewish-Roman war of AD 135 Bar Cocheba (Son of the Star) claimed to be the Messiah. Many interpreters believe there will be a supreme manifestation of Antichrist in the end time. They cite Paul's reference to "the man of lawlessness . . . the son of perdition," who proclaims himself to be God (2 Thess. 2:3-8). They also identify the Antichrist with the first beast of Revelation (13:1f; 20:10).

Although John did not deny a supreme manifestation of antichrist, undoubtedly he referred to the Gnostic teachers of his day. Verse 19 suggests that these false teachers once belonged to the Christian community to which John and his readers belonged. Yet the Gnostics were not true members because they had left the Christian community. Despite the Gnostics' claim to spiritual truth, not they but the other members really knew God since they had been "anointed by the Holy One" (v. 20). Although the "Holy One" may refer to God the Father, the Son, or the Holy Spirit, the term *Christ* means Anointed One. In the Old Testament, we learn that prophets, priests, and kings were anointed before assuming office. Jesus fulfilled all three of these offices or roles. He was the supreme spokesman for God, the perfect high priest who gave himself as the perfect sacrifice, and is the "King of kings and Lord of lords" (Rev. 19:16).

Whereas John's readers knew the truth (v. 21), the Gnostics were liars because they denied that Jesus was the Christ or Messiah (v. 22*a*). In denying both the Son and the Father, the Gnostics identified themselves as antichrists (v. 22*b*). The unity of the Father and the Son is such that to deny one is to deny the other, and to confess one is to confess the other (v. 23).

God's Indwelling Word and Spirit (2:24-27)

In order to resist the gnostic heresy, the Christians needed two things: (1) God's abiding Word and (2) God's abiding Spirit. Verse 24 refers particularly to the gospel which the readers had "heard from the beginning." Consequently, to abide in the gospel is to "abide in the Son and in the Father." Jesus effectively appealed to God's Word in resisting the temptations at the outset of his ministry (Matt. 4:1-11). God's Word for the Christian soldier is both an offensive (Eph. 6:17) and a defensive weapon (Ps. 119:11). Moreover, the gospel is the means that God uses to produce spiritual children (Rom. 1:16; Jas. 1:18; 1 Pet. 1:23). Those who have God's abiding Word possess "eternal life" (v. 25), which is both quantitative (lasts forever) and qualitative (lived in fellowship with God).

The "anointing" (*chrisma*) refers to the Holy Spirit (v. 27). John the Baptist had predicted that Jesus would baptize with the Holy Spirit (Matt. 3:11). According to Acts 1:5, this prophecy found fulfillment in the outpouring of the Holy Spirit at Pentecost. Because a person cannot be saved apart from the convicting and illuminating power of the Holy Spirit, the Holy Spirit takes up his abode in us at conversion and from then on is our constant companion, helper, and teacher promised by Jesus (John 15:26; 16:13-15). In contrast to the false teachers (v. 26), John's readers had the Holy Spirit as their teacher who would always teach them the truth (v. 27).

Living in Christ (2:28-29)

Although John used personal pronouns in such a way that we cannot always tell whether he specifically meant the Father, Son, or Holy Spirit, apparently he referred to Christ in verses 28-29. Perhaps John did not have the problem of understanding the triune nature of God as we have. He thus moved with ease back and forth from the unity to the diversity of God. John exhorted his readers to "abide in him" (v. 28a). In so doing John echoed the teaching of Jesus (John 15:1-11). Abiding in Christ involves a mystical union, yet not to the extent that the believer's personality is absorbed. Rather, in union with Christ we actualize our real humanity and full potential as persons.

Apparently, we abide in Christ to the extent that we submit to his control of our lives on a daily, hour by hour, basis. When Jesus returns, some will have "confidence," or boldness, while others will be ashamed or disappointed "at his coming" (v. 28b). No doubt the worldly Christian will feel a deep sense of guilt in the glorious presence of Christ. Jesus urged his disciples to be ready and to be working in view of his sudden return (Matt. 25:1-30). John reminded his readers that their knowledge of Christ as righteous meant that they also knew that those "born of him" must practice righteousness (v. 29).

Children of God

3:1 to 5:12

Characterized by Privilege and Hope (3:1-3)

John called attention to the believers' high privilege of being called "children of God" (v. 1a). Since only those who know God are his children, the "world" does not recognize Christians as children of God (v. 1b). Peter implied this truth as he defended himself before the Sanhedrin (Acts 5:29-32).

Being children of God includes a beginning, a process of growth, and a consummation or maturity. As "sons of God," we are in a gradual process of realizing the nature and character of Christ (2 Cor. 3:18; Eph. 4:13). As Nathaniel Hawthorne fittingly depicted in his story, "The Great Stone Face," we tend to become like our ideal. Although Moses could not see the fullness of God (Ex. 33:12-23), when Christ returns "we shall be like him, for we shall see him as he is" (v. 2). Of course, we shall not be totally like Christ, but throughout eternity we shall continue to grow toward his marvelous perfection. Everyone who has the hope of Christ's return and to be like him "purifies himself as he is pure" (v. 3). This purifying process is known as sanctification.

Characterized by Righteousness (3:4-10)

John rejected both the gnostic belief in sinless perfection (1:8,10) and the argument of those who thought that giving themselves to sinful passions did not matter. The apostle equated sin and lawlessness (v. 4). By "lawlessness" the author meant antinomianism, the view that certain people are not subject to moral law. Because Jesus came the first time "to take away sins" and he himself is sinless (v. 5), the necessary conclusion is that anyone "who abides in him" does not characteristically or habitually sin (v. 6). John, of course, did not contradict what he had written earlier. Rather, he was dealing with a different problem. For example, John refuted ascetic, sinless perfectionists by saying that those who claim they do not sin or have not sinned deceive themselves (1:8) and make God a liar (1:10). Here he refuted the libertine (antinomian) Gnostics by showing that sin cannot be characteristic of Christians just as it is not characteristic of Christ.

John tenderly appealed to his readers not to be deceived by such false teachers by pointing out that righteous conduct reveals righteous character, like that of Christ (v. 7). On the contrary, the person "who commits sin is of the devil," since sin has always been characteristic of the devil (v. 8a). The purpose of Christ's first advent (the incarnation) was "to destroy the works of the devil" (v. 8b).

Jesus' climactic defeat of the devil was at the cross (John 12:31).

Boldly asserting that "No one born of God commits sin," John supported his assertion by adding, "for God's nature abides in him, and he cannot sin because he is born of God" (v. 9). Although the Revised Standard Version does not give a literal translation, it may be correct in its interpretation. The word for "nature" actually is "seed" and is rendered "offspring" by some, including the alternate reading of the Revised Standard Version. According to the latter, God's "offspring" abide in him and thus cannot sin. Others believe that "seed" refers to the gospel or God's Word, which is God's means of begetting spiritual children (Jas. 1:18; 1 Pet. 1:23). Jesus appealed to God's Word when he was faced with temptation (Matt. 4:4,7,10), and the psalmist wrote, "I have laid up thy word in my heart, that I might not sin against thee" (Ps. 119:11). Those who divide man into two parts, the spiritual and the physical, and claim that the born-again part of the believer cannot sin, although his fleshly part can, fall into the same deception of the antinomian Gnostics whom John was refuting. In favor of "nature" is Jesus' statement to Nicodemus, "That which is born of the flesh is flesh, and that which is born of the Spirit is spirit" (John 3:6).

How can we distinguish between children of God and children of the devil? According to John both their life-styles and their attitudes are different. In contrast to the righteous life-style of God's children, the devil's children do not practice righteousness; neither do they demonstrate love for others (v. 10).

Characterized by Love (3:11-18)

John's readers had "heard from the beginning" that they "should love one another" (v. 11). Likely he had taught them Jesus' words, "By this all men will know that you are my disciples, if you have love for one another" (John 13:35). John cited Cain as an example of the devil's children because he failed to demonstrate love toward his brother Abel but killed him instead, thus proving that "his own deeds were evil and his brother's righteous" (v. 12). When John added, "Do not wonder, brethren, that the world hates you" (v. 13), he echoed the warning of Jesus (John 15:18).

According to verse 14, "We know that we have passed out of death into life, because we love the brethren," while in contrast, "He who does not love abides in death." The opposite of love is hate, and "Any one who hates his brother is a murderer" (v. 15*a*). Like Jesus, John stressed the motive behind the overt act. When John added, "and you know that no murderer has eternal life abiding in him" (v. 15*b*), he did not mean that murder is an unforgivable sin, since a forgiven murderer is no longer a murderer in God's sight. John's point is that hatred (murder) is a sign that the person who hates is not a child of God.

Perhaps coincidentally, 1 John 3:16 complements John 3:16. God's supreme demonstration of love as expressed in John 3:16 is the model for our love for others. However, Paul wrote that few people are willing to die for the very best of persons (Rom. 5:7). In verses 17-18, John insisted that love involves loving deeds, not merely an attitude of goodwill or pious expressions. Genuine love involves sharing material possessions with the needy because we really care for them.

Characterized by Assurance and Obedience (3:19-24)

In verse 14, John had indicated that Christians may be assured of their salvation because they love other believers. Now he turned to a different line of evidence. According to verses 19-20, our salvation does not depend on our feelings, but on God. When sin in our lives causes us to doubt our salvation, we need to remember that "God is greater than our hearts, and he knows everything," including the fact that we really love him. On the other hand, "if our hearts do not condemn us, we have confidence before God" in prayer (v. 21). The result is that God answers our prayer positively by granting us "whatever we ask, because we keep his commandments and do what pleases him" (v. 22). Although the language seems to suggest that God gives us a number of blank checks for us to fill in the amount, elsewhere we learn that if we pray selfishly, God does not grant our requests (Jas. 4:3).

God's commandment is twofold: (1) to "believe in the name of his Son Jesus Christ" and (2) to "love one another" as Jesus "commanded us" (v. 23). According to John 6:29, Jesus said, "This is the work of God, that you believe in whom he has sent." The necessity of keeping Jesus' commandments (v. 24*a*) also stems from Jesus' words to his disciples (John 14:15; 15:14). Another proof that we are true believers is the abiding presence of the Holy Spirit in our lives (v. 24b; Rom. 5:5; 8:16).

Truth Versus Error (4:1-6)

Since "many false prophets have gone out into the world," there are spirits that Christians need to test "to see whether they are of God" (v. 1). The crucial test is the attitude toward Christ's incarnation (v. 2a). A true spirit confesses the incarnation, whereas a false spirit denies the incarnation and identifies itself as the "spirit of antichrist" (vv. 2b-3). No doubt John had in mind those Gnostic teachers who claimed that the eternal Christ could not become flesh, which they considered evil. John assured his readers that they belonged to God and had overcome the false teachers because God (Christ or Holy Spirit) who indwelt them was "greater than he who is in the world," that is, the devil (v. 4). Because the false teachers were "of the world," they spoke the things of the world and found a ready audience in worldly people (v. 5). On the contrary, Christians are "of God," and those who know God listen to them (v. 6a). Thus, believers are able to "know the spirit of truth and the spirit of error" (v. 6b).

Love's Source and Goal (4:7-12)

John again stressed the importance of love as the main characteristic of Christians. God is the source of love and expects his children to be channels of love to others. God's incarnate Son was the greatest demonstration of divine love and is the source of our life, both physical and spiritual, with emphasis on the latter (v. 9). God, not we, took the initiative in love and "sent his Son to be the expiation for our sins" (v. 10). Because of God's great love for us, "we also ought to love one another" (v. 11). Although no one "has ever seen God," yet "if we love one another, God abides in us and his love is perfected in us" (v. 12). Accordingly, our goal is to become increasingly like God in our love.

Love's Assurance and Demonstration (4:13-21)

John repeated the truth that we can know we are children of God because of his gift of the Holy Spirit (v. 13). Paul wrote that the Holy Spirit is God's earnest or pledge to us that he eventually will complete the salvation he has begun in us (Eph. 1:13-14). John also assured his readers that he and others had actually seen Jesus and thus testified that God had "sent his Son as Savior of the world" (v. 14). Anyone who "confesses that Jesus is the Son of God, God abides in him, and he in God" (v. 15). Contrary to the view that love itself is God, the expression, "God is love," means that love is a personal characteristic of God (v. 16). We may add that God also is holiness, righteousness, and truth. The fact that God is love implies a vital union between the believer and God, joined together by the bond of love.

Perfected love or mature love means "that we may have confidence for the day of judgment" (v. 17a). Unlike those who know not God, believers will have confidence and assurance at the final judgment, not because of their basic goodness but because of their relationship with Christ (God). Just as Christ is God's representative in the world, so are we (v. 17b). Although we are to fear God in the sense of reverential awe, here John used "fear" in the bad sense of terror or fright. Thus, John declared, "There is no fear in love, but perfect love casts out fear" (v. 18a). Mature love so conquers fear that mature Christians may undergo persecution with no fear of their tormentors and with no temptation to compromise their faith in order to avoid suffering (1 Pet. 4:1). The statement that "fear has to do with punishment" (v. 18b) may be contrasted with love, which relates to salvation and reward. The statement also may mean that fear itself produces or essentially includes punishment. Can you imagine the inner torment of elderly people who live in constant fear of being assaulted and robbed, or people who live under the perpetual threat of having the police knock on their door to place them under arrest for imaginary crimes against the state?

Since God is the source of love, "We love, because he first loved us" (v. 19). Without God's initiative, we would never experience or express love. If anyone claims to love God and yet "hates his brother, he is a liar"; it is impossible not to love a visible brother and at the same time love the invisible God (v. 20). The love commandment includes both the vertical (love for God) and the horizontal relationship (love for man) (v. 21).

Love and Triumphant Faith in Christ (5:1-5)

Chapter 5 continues the theme of love for both God and fellow Christians. John began by asserting, "Every one who believes that Jesus is the Christ is a child of God" (v. 1a). "Child of God," is literally "has been begotten by God." The idea is that to love the Heavenly Father automatically means to love his children (v. 1b). Moreover, "By this we know that we love the children of God, when we love God and obey his commandments" (v. 2). If we love God, the necessary consequence is "that we keep his commandments," which "are not burdensome" (v. 3). One reason God's commandments are not burdensome is that he enables us to keep them, although no one keeps them perfectly. "For whatever is born of God overcomes the world" by means of faith (v. 4). Overcoming the world includes overcoming temptations, which God enables us to overcome (1 Cor. 10:13). Faith "that overcomes the world" is not just any sort of faith; it is faith in Jesus as the Son of God (v. 5).

Three Witnesses (5:6-12)

Interpretations of this controversial passage broadly follow three lines. Those who say that the water and the blood refers to baptism and the Lord's Supper as the two church ordinances seem to have at best only a partial truth, since the Lord's Supper just does not fit John's words. Still others seek a symbolic meaning related to the water and blood that came from Jesus' side following the spear thrust (John 19:34). The view that best suits the context holds that water refers to Jesus' baptism when the Holy Spirit came upon him and the heavenly voice expressed God's approval (Matt. 3:16-17). Consequently, blood refers to Jesus' death, prior to which again the divine approval came (John 12:27-30).

Since John earlier refuted the Gnostic teachers, he apparently did so again. One form of gnosticism, later expressed by the gnostic

Cerinthus, insisted that Jesus was born mere man and died mere man. Supposedly, however, God temporarily adopted Jesus at his baptism and forsook him at the cross. Thus, Jesus was the Son of God only for the short interval of some three years between his baptism and his death. By insisting that Jesus Christ came "not with the water only but with the water and the blood" (v. 6), John refuted the Gnostic doctrine by affirming that Jesus was fully the Son of God at the cross as well as at his baptism. Otherwise, his death would not be effective to save from sin. The "three witnesses, the Spirit, the water, and the blood," all agree to the divine sonship of Christ (v. 8). Since people ordinarily accept the truthfulness of human testimony, how much more readily they should accept the testimony of God who (repeatedly) "has borne witness to his Son" (v. 9).

The person "who believes in the Son of God" has the authenticating witness of faith in himself (v. 10*a*; Heb. 11:1). In addition, he has the inner testimony of the Holy Spirit. Contrariwise, the person (like the Gnostics) who rejects God's witness concerning his Son in effect has made God "a liar" (v. 10*b*). God's testimony includes the truth "that God gave us eternal life, and this life is in his Son" (v. 11). In the final analysis, "He who has the Son has life; he who has not the Son of God has not life" (v. 12). There is no neutral position, for neutrality toward Christ amounts to rejection, thus no spiritual life.

Final Counsel
5:13-21

Assurance and Expectant Prayer (5:13-15)

Verse 13 states the central purpose of the epistle, that the readers may know they have eternal life. Such assurance encourages Christians to pray boldly and expectantly (v. 14). Not only does God hear our prayers, but "we know that we have obtained the requests made of him" (v. 15). You will note in verse 14 an all-important condition of prayer, "according to his will." This condition rules out selfish prayer. We need to avoid two extremes in prayer: (1) making selfish demands on God and (2) asking timidly with no real expectancy that God will grant our requests.

The Sin unto Death (5:16-17)

The problem of "mortal sin" or literally "sin unto death" is perhaps the most difficult issue raised in the entire letter. Interpreters have offered basically three different views of the sin unto death: (1) A specific but undetermined sin, (2) apostasy or falling away from faith in Christ, and (3) the unpardonable sin or blasphemy against the Holy Spirit. Early in church history the Roman Catholic Church used this passage to support a doctrine of mortal sins, that is, sins that result in spiritual death. To lesser sins Catholics apply the designation "venial sins." Such a distinction, however, seems artificial and contrived. Because John used the term "brother," some view the sin unto death as apostasy and refer to similar passages like Hebrews 6:4-8; 10:26-31; and James 5:19-20. Yet such a view seems to contradict John's earlier statement that a person born of God cannot sin (3:9). If John referred to blasphemy against the Holy Spirit, the person he had in mind was an unbeliever, but why did he use the word "brother"? John ordinarily used the word "brother" or "brethren" to refer to a fellow believer or believers. In his reference to Cain, John used "brother" to mean a physical brother or sibling (3:11). Some interpreters believe that John also used "brother" to designate fellow human beings, for example, his usage in 2:9-11. In the strictest sense, however, John did not say that a brother may sin unto death. At most he merely implied it when he wrote, "There is sin which is mortal" (v. 16).

If we interpret death to mean physical instead of spiritual death, we have two other possible interpretations. First, John might have referred to cases like that of Ananias and Sapphira (Acts 5:1-11) and Paul's implication that some Christians in Corinth had died because of their abuse of the Lord's Supper (1 Cor. 11:30). On the other hand, John might have meant a Christian who so sins that his sin will stigmatize him as long as he lives, for example, a minister who has an affair with another woman. However, against both of these views is the fact that John used a word for life which he elsewhere consistently used to mean spiritual life. In conclusion, we may add that blasphemy against the Holy Spirit is the interpretation that seems to have the fewest problems. Since we cannot certainly know when a person has committed the sin unto death, we ought to continue to pray for all sinners.

Victory over Sin (5:18-21)

John concluded his epistle with a strong emphasis on assurance. The first part of verse 18 is similar to 3:9, but the last part is quite different. In 3:9 the believer's life is characterized by sinlessness because of the indwelling "nature" (seed), while here it is because of the sustaining presence of Christ. The Revised Standard Version's "but He who was born of God keeps him" better renders the original than "but he that is begotten of God keepeth himself" (KJV). Although there is a sense in which believers keep them-selves, the initiative and real keeping rest with Christ who said of his followers, "and I give them eternal life, and they shall never perish, and no one shall snatch them out of my hand" (John 10:28). The additional assurance, "the evil one does not touch him" (v. 18b), means not that the believer will never be tempted, but that Satan can never cause permanent harm to a Christian.

While Christians have the assurance of knowing that they are God's children, in contrast, "the whole world is in the power of the evil one" (v. 19). God's permissive will allows Satan to dominate the minds of those who misuse their freedom of choice to follow Satan rather than God.

Contrary to the false knowledge of the Gnostics, believers "know that the Son of God has come and has given us understanding, to know him who is true" (v. 20a). Not only has Christ come in the incarnation, but, he abides in us spiritually as our constant compan-ion and helper (John 14:16-18). Christ makes God the Father known to us. As believers, we are in both the Father and the Son (v. 20b) just as Jesus requested in his high priestly prayer (John 17:20-21). The last part of verse 20 reiterates Jesus' words in John 17:3, "And this is eternal life, that they know thee the only true God, and Jesus Christ whom thou hast sent."

The parting words, "Little children keep yourselves from idols" (v. 21), on the surface may seem like an odd way to end this epistle.

Yet we must remember that any sort of substitute for God, whether material or mental, is an idol. Perhaps John referred particularly to the false system of knowledge advocated by the Gnostics. Since we belong to God, any flirtation with the world or with false teaching is spiritual adultery, or idolatry, and thus violates the First Commandment: "You shall have no other gods before me" (Ex. 20:3).

2 JOHN

Personal Greeting (1-3)

The author identified himself as "The elder." Although the word "elder" may simply refer to an older person, here it clearly seems to be an official title (Acts 14:23). While some make a distinction between elder, bishop, and pastor, a careful study of all New Testament occurrences seems to indicate that the three terms are used interchangeably. That apostles were sometimes called elders is shown by 1 Peter 5:1, as Peter referred to himself as a "fellow elder." The expression, "to the elect lady and her children," may refer either to a Christian woman and her children or to a church and its members. The overall content of the letter seems to favor the latter view. The word "elect" means "chosen" and refers to God's initiative in salvation.

John jointly expressed his love together with "all who know the truth," no doubt meaning the truth of the gospel as expressed in the incarnation, death, and resurrection of Christ. This same truth, which contrasted with the falsehood of the Gnostic teachers, "abides in us and will be with us for ever" (v. 2a). We could scarcely wish for a stronger statement of the believer's eternal security.

To the usual "Grace" and "peace," John added the word "mercy" (v. 3a). The basic meaning of grace is favor, and in the New Testament it usually refers to divine favor, thus undeserved favor. The word translated "peace" is the Greek equivalent of the familiar Hebrew *shalom*, which basically means wholeness: physical, mental, and spiritual. Mercy is a sort of combination of love and pity, and, like divine love, it always seeks the best for its object. Instead of the usual "to you," John confidently predicted that "Grace, mercy, and peace will be with us." The source of these spiritual benefits is "God the Father and . . . Jesus Christ the Father's Son" (v. 3b). Truth as in the expression, "truth and love," means ultimate reality, that which is permanently real and lasting, thus spiritual in contrast with the physical.

Living in Truth and Love (4-6)

John revealed his delight in the spiritual progress of the church as he wrote, "I rejoiced greatly to find some of your children following the truth" (v. 4). Perhaps "those of your children" would better express John's statement than "some of your children." Using language similar to that of 1 John (1:7; 3:11), John encouraged the church to obey the love commandment, which was not a "new commandment," the essence of which is to "love one another" (v. 5). Verse 6 in effect repeats the content of verse 5. In both verses, references to "the beginning" apparently denote the outset of the Christian movement. Love has always been the single outstanding characteristic of Jesus and his followers (John 13:35).

Warning Against False Teachers (7-11)

Almost certainly the "many deceivers" of verse 7 were Gnostic teachers that John condemned in his first letter. Only here and in 1 John (2:18,22; 4:3) do we find the term "antichrist," which means one who opposes Christ or who substitutes himself for Christ, perhaps both. Those who bore the brunt of John's condemnation were the Docetic Gnostics who denied that the eternal Christ could or did become flesh. John issued a stern warning as he wrote, "Look to yourselves, that you may not lose what you have worked for, but may win a full reward" (v. 8). Contrary to the view that John was afraid his readers might lose their salvation if they accepted the Gnostic view of Christ, he seemingly referred to spiritual development as shown by the added words, "but may win a full reward." Yet John bluntly warned, "Any one who goes ahead and does not abide in the doctrine of Christ does not have God" (v. 9a). On the contrary, "he who abides in the doctrine has both the Father and the Son" (v. 9b). By "doctrine of Christ," John, of course, meant the doctrine of God become flesh in the person of Jesus Christ. Only those who have the Son have life (1 John 5:12).

Verses 10-11 concern giving hospitality to itinerant Gnostic teachers. Hospitality was characteristic of the early Christians just as it was of the Old Testament patriarchs. Hospitality involved fellowship and implied acceptance of one another. Yet John saw the

Gnostic teaching as such a danger to the Christian faith that he dealt
with the Gnostics as severely as Paul did with the Judaizers (Gal.
1:6-9). Thus, he urged his readers neither to give a false teacher
hospitality nor to "give him any greeting; for he who greets him
shares his wicked work" (vv. 10-11). As we face the problem of how
to deal with cultists who come to our door in their propagandizing
efforts, we need to observe two principles: (1) not to be unloving
and rude and (2) not to compromise our integrity by condoning
their false teachings. Above all, we must be sure that we do not
encourage false teachers or weaken our Christian faith and witness.

Concluding Words (12-13)

John indicated that he had much more to write, but he preferred
to speak with them "face to face" (literally, "mouth to mouth")
rather than to "use paper and ink." His stated reason for seeing
them is expressed in the words "that our joy may be complete."
Though he might have used "our" merely in the editorial sense,
John likely included his readers in his wish for perfect joy. If the
"elect lady" of verse 1 designated a church, then "elect sister" must
necessarily refer to a sister church, and her "children" would be the
church members. Otherwise, in both instances John meant Christian women and their children.

3 JOHN

Greeting and Approval of Gaius (1-4)

As we noted in 2 John, the writer identified himself as "The elder," but this title does not rule out his apostleship. The Gaius to whom the letter was addressed is not otherwise identified. If not the pastor, he probably was a leading layman in the church. Acts 19:29 mentions a Macedonian Gaius who was Paul's traveling companion. Also, there was a "Gaius of Derbe" (Acts 20:4) and a Gaius of Corinth (1 Cor. 1:14), who is probably the same Gaius mentioned in Romans 16:23. A warmer greeting could scarcely have been given, as indicated by the word "beloved" and the additional "whom I love in the truth." John expressed concern for Gaius' health as well as confidence that his spiritual condition was sound (v. 2). John had "greatly rejoiced" on receiving a report from certain "brethren" who had testified to Gaius's spiritual integrity, and John had heartily agreed with their testimony (v. 3). To "follow the truth" (vv 3-4) means to live according to the example and teachings of Christ. John could think of "No greater joy" than "to hear that my children follow the truth" (v. 4). Of course, he meant spiritual, not physical, children.

Request for Christian Hospitality (5-8)

Although John in his second epistle warned his readers not to extend hospitality to false teachers, here he commended Gaius for being hospitable "to the brethren, especially to strangers, who have testified to your love before the church" (vv. 5-6a). He then added, "You will do well to send them on their journey as befits God's service" (v. 6b). No doubt John referred to itinerant Christian missionaries. For example, Paul frequently was a guest in Christian homes (Acts 16:15; 18:2-3). The purpose of the missionaries' travels was for "his sake," that is, Christ's sake (v. 7a). When John explained that the missionaries had "accepted nothing from the heathen [Gentiles]," he clearly meant pagans or "heathen," since converted Gentiles were no longer pagans but children of God (v. 7b). Christians have both a moral obligation to help and the privilege to be "fellow workers in the truth" when they extend hospitality and other aid to traveling missionaries (v. 8).

Criticism of Diotrephes (9-10)

The identity of Diotrephes is not clear. Some believe that he, not Gaius, was the pastor. Otherwise, he must have been a prominent layman. Since the early churches usually seemed to have more than one elder or pastor, possibly both Gaius and Diotrephes were pastors. At any rate, John described Diotrephes as one "who likes to put himself first" and who "does not acknowledge my authority" (v. 9). Reference to the writer's authority suggests that the "elder" was none other than the apostle John. Moreover, the writer implied that his authority was greater than that of Diotrephes whom, if the author should come, he would call into account for his "prating against me with evil words" (v. 10a). In addition, Diotrephes had refused hospitality to the traveling missionaries whom he had expelled from the church (v. 10b). Since the missionaries would not have been members of that particular congregation, the words "puts them out of the church" probably do not refer to excommunication but to expulsion from the meeting place, perhaps a home or a borrowed or rented building. Whether because of wealth, social prestige, or for some other reasons, Diotrephes played a dictator role in the church.

Praise for Demetrius (11-12)

After encouraging Gaius not to imitate evil but good, he concluded by saying that "He who does good is of God; he who does evil has not seen God" (v. 11). This statement reminds us of 1 John 3:7-8 and also of Jesus' statement: "So, every sound tree bears good fruit, but the bad tree bears evil fruit" (Matt. 7:17). Ethical behavior is a clear indicator of one's character. Undoubtedly John meant to contrast Demetrius with Diotrephes. Consequently, he praised

Demetrius who had a threefold witness of his moral integrity: (1) "from every one," (2) "from the truth itself," and (3) from John (v. 12). Probably Demetrius was the bearer of the letter. Since the church to which Gaius belonged was in Asia, there is at least a remote possibility that this Demetrius was the same as Demetrius, the silversmith of Ephesus, who vehemently opposed Paul and his Christian companions (Acts 19:24,38). However, there is no indication in Acts concerning the conversion of Demetrius.

Concluding Remarks (13-15)

In words similar to his farewell remarks in 2 John, the author indicated that he had much more to write; but instead of writing with "pen and ink," he hoped to see Gaius soon so they could "talk together face to face" (vv. 13-14). John next wished Gaius well by writing, "Peace be to you," then adding, "The friends greet you. Greet the friends, every one of them" (v. 15). Wherever John was at the time, he was in the presence of Christian friends.

JUDE

Introduction

Although it is a brief letter of only twenty-five verses, Jude makes a significant contribution to the early Christian literature that refutes the false doctrine of a group generally believed to be Gnostics. The epistles 2 Peter, 1 John, and 2 John also combat this gnostic teaching. The central tenet of gnosticism was the concept of the essential goodness of spirit and the evil of matter. Accordingly, God could not, and did not, become flesh in the person of Jesus Christ. From the standpoint of morality, the Gnostics divided into two opposite positions. One group attempted to subdue the flesh by ascetic practices, sometimes to the extreme of abusing their bodies. The other group attempted to pacify the body by giving in to all appetites, with the excuse that the body, being evil, did not matter anyway. Jude clearly refuted the doctrines and practices of the latter group, also known as antinomians or libertines.

Even a casual reading of 2 Peter and Jude reveals a remarkable similarity. Interpreters generally have taken one of three positions: (1) Peter borrowed from Jude; (2) Jude borrowed from Peter; (3) both Peter and Jude used a common source. Although establishing the fact that Peter and Jude wrote about the identical group of false teachers is impossible, undoubtedly both wrote about the same problem.

Questions concerning the canonicity of 2 Peter and Jude arose in the early years of the church, mainly because both writers quoted with approval from nonbiblical (apocryphal) sources. Some of the early church fathers wanted to canonize the apocryphal books on the basis that two inspired writers quoted from them. On the other hand, others tended to reject the authenticity of 2 Peter and Jude because they quoted from nonbiblical sources. Two other positions are possible. For example, the Holy Spirit could have inspired Peter and Jude to quote only portions of the apocryphal writings that were true. Also, Peter and Jude could have used the apocryphal sources as illustrations without affirming their truthfulness.

The identity of Jude is not certainly established. The New Testament refers to six different men who had the name of Jude or Judas. They are: (1) Judas Iscariot; (2) "Judas the son of James" (possibly a brother), also called Thaddeus, one of the twelve (Matt. 10:3; Luke 6:16); (3) Judas the brother of Jesus (Matt 13:55); (4) Judas of Galilee (Acts 5:37); (5) Judas of Damascus (Acts 9:11); and (6) Judas Barsabbas, a Christian from Jerusalem (Acts 15:22). Because the author identified himself as "Jude . . . brother of James" (v. 1), tradition has concluded that Jude was the brother (or half-brother) of Jesus. No valid reason to doubt the traditional authorship of Jude has been found.

Since the letter is very brief, there is not sufficient evidence to establish the date of composition. Interpreters have assigned dates from as early as AD 60 to AD 140. The latter extreme, of course, would rule out Jude, the brother of Jesus, as author. Any date that allows for traditional authorship is acceptable and creates no real problems concerning authenticity.

Salutation
1-2

As customary in ancient letters, the writer introduced himself at the beginning rather than the end of his letter. Some interpreters believe that Jude surely would have introduced himself as Jesus' brother, instead of "servant of Jesus Christ," if he actually had been Jesus' brother. Jude, however, could have intended to reflect modesty as well as his recognition of Jesus' lordship. The term "servant" means bond servant or bond slave, thus a slave attached to his master for life. Further identification as "brother of James" seems to mean James, the brother of Jesus, who succeeded Peter as leader of the Jerusalem church (Acts 15:13-21; 21:18).

Jude addressed himself "To those who are called, beloved in God the Father and kept for Jesus Christ." Another possibility is to substitute "by God" for "in God" and "in Jesus Christ" instead of "for Jesus Christ." Since Jude did not include a place name, we cannot identify his readers. However, the Gnostic heresy was prevalent in the Roman province of Asia. Like Paul, Jude no doubt used "called" in the sense, not of those merely invited, but of those who had actually accepted the invitation to become disciples of Jesus Christ. Jude wished for his readers an increase of "mercy, peace, and love." In the context, mercy seems to denote God's compassionate concern. The basic meaning of "peace" is wholeness, including the physical, mental, and spiritual areas of life. "Love" denotes divine love, which is self-giving and always includes positive goodwill toward its object.

A Plea for Sound Doctrine
3-4

Interpreters generally agree that Jude originally intended to write a letter concerning the mutual body of Christian teachings, but diverted his attention toward the Gnostic heresy because of its imminent threat. The expression "common salvation" does not mean ordinary salvation. Rather, it means salvation held jointly or in common. Although the word *faith* usually designates personal commitment in scriptural usage, here it has the definite article and clearly seems to refer to a body of Christian teachings or doctrines. The description, "once for all delivered to the saints," further underscores the view that Jude referred to an established body of teachings. For example, the word translated "once for all" means once for all time, and the word rendered "delivered" designates something passed on by one generation to another and in noun form is the basis for the word *tradition*.

Verse 4 introduces the problem group who had "secretly gained" admission into the Christian community. The further description that they "long ago were designated for this condemnation" may refer to apostolic warnings, (2 Pet. 3:2f.) and perhaps to warnings in the nonbiblical book of 1 Enoch (vv. 14-15). Their sins included impiety or godlessness together with the perversion of God's grace into "licentiousness" or sensuality. Jude further characterized the heretics with the accusation that they "deny our only Master and

Lord, Jesus Christ." Perhaps they denied Christ in two senses:
(1) by rejecting his deity and (2) by living sinful lives contrary to his
teaching (2 Pet. 2:1).

A Warning Against False Doctrine
5-16

The Lesson from History (5-9)

In verses 5-7, Jude reminded his readers of three examples which
illustrate the truth that God's nature is such that he cannot condone
sin but, rather, must punish it. The first example was that of the
disobedient Israelites who had enough faith to leave Egypt but not
enough to enter the Promised Land. They resultantly perished
during forty years of wilderness wandering (Num. 14:26-35). Next
Jude reminded them of the rebellious angels who now were "kept
by him in eternal chains in the nether gloom until the judgment of
the great day." Like Peter (2 Pet. 2:4), Jude apparently derived this
information from 1 Enoch. Later the English poet, John Milton, in
Paradise Lost used his imagination to give a detailed account of the
rebellion and expulsion of Satan and his angels from heaven. Jude's
third illustration was the destruction of "Sodom and Gomorrah and
the surrounding cities" (Gen. 19:24-25). The expression "unnatural
lust" literally means "other flesh" or flesh of a different kind from
God's intention, thus males having sexual relationships with one
another.

Jude put the libertine Gnostics in the same category as the three
groups he had just described (v. 8). The expression "their dream-
ings" may refer to the Gnostics' claim of divine revelation (Acts
2:17). Accordingly, Jude refuted their claim by insisting that God-
inspired people do not live immoral lives. The two characteristic
sins were sensual living and rejection of authority. For example, the
Israelites commited immoral acts in the golden calf incident as well
as on other occasions. They also rejected both the authority of God
and Moses. Although Jude wrote nothing about the sensuality of the

fallen angels, their rebellion against God's authority is obvious. The men of Sodom lived immorally and not only rejected the authority of God's two angels but also attempted to abuse them (Gen. 19:4-11). However, there is no indication that the Sodomites recognized the identity of the angels. Exactly how the Gnostics reviled (blasphemed) "glorious ones" is not clear. Since the Mosaic law was mediated by angels (Gal. 3:19), by rejecting its authority the Gnostics perhaps reviled "glorious ones" (literally, "glories"). On the other hand, Jude might have referred to the Gnostics' rejection of God-given apostolic authority. To illustrate the Gnostics' rebellion against authority, Jude referred to an incident apparently taken from the nonbiblical book, *The Assumption of Moses*. Accordingly, the archangel Michael disputed with the devil over the body of Moses (v. 9). Jude's point was that Michael, unlike the Gnostics, recognized the authority of the devil and thus did not directly rebuke him, but, rather, appealed to God's higher authority for rebuke.

Description of the False Teachers (10-16)

Jude compared the Gnostic heretics with "irrational animals" who eventually would be destroyed by the authority they blasphemed (v. 10). Thus, their sin carried within it the seeds of destruction. Jude compared them with Cain who was condemned to a life of wandering after he had murdered his brother Abel (Gen. 4:12). He further compared them with greedy Balaam (Num. 22:4f.), and Korah who rebelled against Moses and Aaron and later perished when he and his followers fell into a crevice in the earth (Num. 16:1f.).

Next Jude described the heretics as "blemishes [perhaps "reefs" or "rocks"] on your love feasts, as they bodily carouse together" (v. 12a). Apparently Jude referred to gluttonous meals that demonstrated selfishness instead of love, perhaps eaten in the context of the Lord's Supper (1 Cor. 11:17-22). Continuing his condemnation, Jude characterized the false teachers as "waterless clouds, carried about by winds," thus failing in their God-given purpose to sustain life (v. 12b). Moreover, they were like "fruitless trees in late autumn, twice dead, uprooted" (v. 12c), thus utterly useless and unproductive, like the fruitless fig tree Jesus condemned (Matt. 21:18-19). As "wild waves of the sea," and "wandering stars," the Gnostic heretics could never enjoy spiritual rest and stood condemned since they served no useful purpose in life (v. 13).

Jude found in the book of 1 Enoch an appropriate statement of the eventual judgment of wicked people like the false teachers (vv. 14-15). The "holy myriads" (ten thousands) refer to angelic beings as executors of divine judgment. Jesus made a similar statement when he said, "When the Son of man comes in his glory and all the angels with him" (Matt. 25:31). Finally, Jude characterized the Gnostics as "grumblers, malcontents, following their own passions, loud-mouthed boasters, flattering people to gain advantage" (v. 16).

Encouragement to Faithfulness
17-23

After a lengthy digression to warn his readers against the Gnostic heretics, Jude apparently returned to the subject of "the faith which was once for all delivered to the saints," begun in verse 3. This body of apostolic writings included "predictions" that "In the last time there will be scoffers, following their own ungodly passions" (vv. 17-18). Although Jude did not disclose the subject of the scoffers, Peter indicated that it concerned Christ's second coming (2 Pet. 3:1-10). According to Jude, the scoffers were divisive, worldly, and unspiritual (v. 19).

In contrast to the factious nature of the scoffers, Jude referred to the readers as "beloved" and encouraged them to "build yourselves up on your most holy faith" and to "pray in the Holy Spirit" (v. 20). Prayer in the Holy Spirit involves being guided by the Holy Spirit who is the great intercessor for believers (Rom. 8:26-27). Studying God's Word, mutual sharing and encouragement, and witnessing to God's saving grace are other ways of spiritual development. In addition, Jude urged the Christian community to keep themselves in God's love and to "wait for the mercy of our Lord Jesus Christ unto eternal life" (v. 21). In contrast to the judgment upon the false teachers, the believers could assuredly expect mercy. By "eternal life" Jude referred not to the beginning of eternal life but to its climax and fulfillment at Christ's return

Despite textual problems with verses 22-23, Jude clearly seemed to refer to three groups, perhaps all affected in varying degrees by the Gnostics' false teaching. Some interpreters take all three groups to refer to genuine, though weak, Christians, while others identify only the first group as such. Apparently the doubters were partially convinced that the Gnostics' teachings were correct. Consequently, Jude urged the stronger Christians to convince the doubters of the wrongness of the Gnostic doctrine and the rightness of the true body of Christian teaching. The second group had an even stronger leaning toward the false teaching. They seemingly were on the verge of full acceptance and thus were in danger of the "fire" of divine judgment. Others interpret "fire" to mean temptations related to sexual immorality, which was characteristic of the libertine teachers. Finally, the third group apparently had fully succumbed to the heretical teaching. The expression, "have mercy with fear, hating even the garment spotted by the flesh," may be Jude's way of saying that they should love sinners but hate their sins. Like Paul in his dealing with the problem of the Judaizers, Jude never actually said that believers could lose their salvation. Reference to "the garment spotted by the flesh," as well as "snatching them out of the fire," may allude to Zechariah 3:2-5. However, the concept of a contaminated garment better fits the danger of a garment infected with leprosy. Consequently, sin is moral leprosy.

Doxology
24-25

Jude's epistle closes with an unusually beautiful and meaningful doxology. He commended his readers "to him who is able to keep you from falling," that is, to God, who is able to keep them from yielding to temptation, whether related to false teaching or otherwise. God also is able to complete the salvation that he has begun in them (Phil. 1:6) as shown in the words, "to present you without blemish before the presence of his glory with rejoicing." God also is "Savior" or Deliverer from sin "through Jesus Christ our Lord." To God [as well as Christ] belongs "glory, majesty, dominion, and authority" throughout all eternity.

REVELATION

Introduction

Unfortunately, more controversy centers around the interpretation of Revelation than any other book of the Bible. Those who take the so-called literal approach (that the Bible says what it means and means what it says) conclude that one day horselike creatures will appear, having lionlike heads that emit fire, smoke, and brimstone, and also having snakelike heads that inflict hurt on evil men (Rev. 9:16-19). Yet the same interpreters probably forsake their literal stance when they interpret Jesus' words "Take, eat; this is my body" (Matt. 26:26) or his words concerning Herod Antipas: "Go and tell that fox" (Luke 13:32). Although the author clearly drew from a vast store of Old Testament figures of speech, one writer has concluded that the keys to interpretation have been lost, the result being that we can only guess at the meaning. While it may be conceded that the original readers probably understood Revelation much better than we do, at the same time we must insist that the central message of Revelation is abundantly clear. Simply stated, Revelation teaches that God and the forces of righteousness are certain to defeat Satan and the forces of evil. In fact, the crucial victory has already been won by Christ at Calvary, and it was authenticated by his glorious resurrection.

Various Approaches

Although some writers list as many as nine major approaches to the interpretation of Revelation, these views may be reduced to four basic approaches, with a fifth consisting of a composite of two or more of the four. The *preterist* (from *preter*, meaning "past") theory claims that the events of Revelation took place in the past. Accordingly, the real enemy of the church was the ancient Roman empire, the antichrist being a Roman emperor (likely Nero or Domitian). This view no doubt is partially correct, but it fails to explain the future element, particularly in chapters 20—22. The opposite of the

51

preterist view is the *futurist* approach. According to the latter, everything beyond chapter 3 concerns not the immediate future but the remote future, that is, the future of the end time. Consequently, the obvious references to Rome refer not to the Rome of the first century but to a rebuilt Rome of the end time, and the Antichrist refers to the political ruler of the rejuvenated Roman empire. Although the futurist approach seems more appropriate than the preterist to explain chapters 20—22, it obviously would have meant very little to the original readers, who were persecuted by first-century Rome.

The *continuous-historical* or *historicist* approach somewhat combines the preterist and the futurist views, but in doing so it creates more problems than it solves. According to this view, Revelation is concerned with the unfolding history of the church. Thus, its proponents tend to view the Roman Catholic Church as the real enemy of true believers, with the personal Antichrist being the pope. Perhaps this view made sense to Protestants during the Reformation and the subsequent Inquisition, but it makes little sense today except for those who believe the end-time Roman empire will be in partnership with the Roman Catholic Church, to be identified with the second beast, which resembled a lamb (Rev. 13:11). The advantage of the *idealist* or *philosophy of history* approach is that you can eat your cake and still have it, so to speak. According to this view, Revelation presents the ongoing conflict between good and evil, which is characteristic of all ages of history. For example, there have been, and will continue to be, many antichrists and many Armageddons. Perhaps the prototype of antichrist was Antiochus Epiphanes, who sacrificed a pig on the altar of Yahweh in the Jewish Temple during the interbiblical period. Other examples may include the Roman emperors Caligula, Nero, Domitian, Trajan, and others, plus still later manifestations in men like Hitler, Tojo, and Stalin.

Having stated the four basic approaches to Revelation, we are proposing a view arbitrarily designated as the *paradoxical* method. Other interpreters call their private view the *historical-exegetical* or some similar label. The approach used in this commentary will include what this writer believes to be the best features of the other four. Since Revelation is a prophecy (Rev. 1:3; 22:7,18-19), like Old Testament prophecies, it has a dual meaning. First, it addresses the problems of its own day, and then it spills over into the future. Put another way, prophecy has both a concrete or physical meaning and an abstract or spiritual meaning. For example, when Hosea wrote, "out of Egypt I called my son" (Hos. 11:1), he referred to the fact that God delivered Israel, personified as God's son, from Egypt during the Exodus. Yet, whether knowingly or unknowingly, Hosea wrote of a greater exodus by Jesus, who would deliver believers not from physical bondage, but from spiritual bondage (Matt. 2:15). Paradoxically, this commentary will seek to so combine the preterist and futurist views that the truth of Revelation will apply both to first-century and twentieth-century Christians.

The Millennial Problem

Regardless of other considerations, one's view of the millennium colors his interpretation of Revelation. While we never achieve perfect objectivity in biblical interpretation, perhaps we tend to be even less objective in our interpretation of Revelation. The term *millennium* derives from two Latin words, *mille* (thousand) and *annum* (year), the resultant meaning being a thousand years. Despite the tremendous impact that millennial views have had on theology, the concept of a thousand-year reign of Christ appears biblically only in Revelation, chapter 20. The three traditional millennial positions are premillennial, postmillennial, and amillennial.

According to the premillennial view, Christ will return before the millennium and then will rule for one thousand years on earth. Assuming a pessimistic view of history, premillennialists believe that society will become increasingly worse until Christ raptures the church and later returns with the saints to rule for a thousand years on earth. As far as we have been able to discover, Papias in the second century was the first interpreter to teach that Christ literally would reign on earth for a thousand years. However, J. A. Bengel, a renowned Greek scholar of the eighteenth century, is recognized as the father of modern premillennialism. A more radical type of premillennialism goes under the label of dispensationalism, originated by J. N. Darby, a preacher of the Plymouth Brethren, in the nineteenth century.

Although possibly derived from Augustine's thought, the newest millennial view is postmillennialism whose founder was Daniel Whitby, a Unitarian, in the eighteenth century. Contrary to the premillennial view, postmillennialists claim the world will become better and better as people increasingly accept the gospel until virtually the entire earth's population will be converted to Christ. After a thousand years of peace on earth, Christ will return, not to rule on earth, but to consummate salvation and judge the wicked, followed by eternity. Popular during the optimistic heyday of the social gospel, the postmillennial view has declined greatly after two world wars, the Korean and Vietnam wars, as well as subsequent and other expression of animosity among nations.

Almost as old as premillennialism, the amillennial view (meaning "no millennium") interprets the millennium figuratively or symbolically rather than literally. Apparently Augustine (AD 354-430) was the first to teach clearly that the millennium was symbolic of the indefinite period of time between the first and the second advents of Christ. Some amillennialists hold the paradoxical view that the world is becoming both better and worse at the same time, depending on one's perspective. Generally speaking, premillennialism and amillennialism are the only two viable options today.

Apocalyptic Literature

The anglicized Greek title for Revelation is *Apocalypse*, which means an unveiling, revealing, or disclosing. However, the term further means an unveiling by means of symbolic language. Apocalyptic literature arose during times of political stress, particularly during the Assyrian and Babylonian crises when Israel played the unenviable role of a captive people. Apocalyptic continued through the Greek and Roman periods. Unlike other literature, apocalyptic literature made use of secret or code language, known to the Hebrews but unknown to their enemies. Both the prophets Ezekiel and Daniel made wide use of apocalyptic language. Later Jesus himself made limited use of apocalyptic language (Matt. 24:29-31; Mark 13:24-27; Luke 21:25-28). However, Revelation is the only complete example of apocalyptic literature in the New Testament.

Fundamental ideas behind all apocalyptic are: (1) the kingship of God, (2) constant conflict between good and evil, (3) divine judgment upon evil, and (4) a philosophy of history to the effect that God is working out his purpose. As indicated above, apocalyptic literature also has a historical basis. In Revelation's case, it was Roman domination and persecution. Other characteristics of apocalyptic literature include its use of symbols, its dramatic quality, its predictive element, and its practicality in terms of giving encouragement to persecuted people. Although most apocalyptic literature was written under an assumed name, usually a famous biblical person like Enoch or Ezra, Revelation was not written under an assumed name. The author claimed to be John, who was exiled to the island of Patmos because of his Christian witness (Rev. 1:9). A very strong Christian tradition holds that the apostle John spent his last years in and around Ephesus and during the emperor Domitian's reign was exiled to Patmos, an island just off the coast from Ephesus. Although the date of writing is uncertain, the approximate date of AD 90-95 seems to fit the limited evidence quite well. Since Domitian was emperor from AD 81-96, the above date, particularly the last years of Domitian's reign, corresponds with his increasing opposition to Christians.

Christ and the Churches
1:1 to 3:22

Prologue (1:1-20)

John introduced and set the stage for his cosmic drama in chapter 1. He clearly and concisely indicated the nature of the writing, its importance, its recipients, its real author and authority, his own situation and part in the writing, and its eternal scope.

Announcement of the Subject (1:1-3)

John immediately identified his work as "The revelation of Jesus Christ" (v. 1a). As a "revelation" (apocalypse), it was a disclosure or unveiling. Its *source* was God; its *subject* was Jesus Christ; and its *purpose* was "to show to his servants what must soon take place" (v. 1b). The verb translated "must take place" indicates a moral and spiritual necessity (John 4:4). The word "soon" (with speed) may mean suddenly or certainly, but not necessarily immediately. Time from God's viewpoint is relative (2 Pet. 3:8). In the clause, "and he made it known by sending his angel to his servant John," Jesus is the antecedent of "he" and thus the intermediate source of the revelation just as he was of creation (John 1:3). The verb "made known" means signified or symbolized. John used the noun form in his Gospel to designate certain of Jesus' miracles which contained a special truth (John 2:11). Although an "angel" (messenger) may be either heavenly or earthly in origin, here it no doubt means the former. John, presumably the apostle, identified himself as a "servant"—actually a slave who was bound to his master for life.

The expression, "who bore witness to the word of God and to the testimony of Jesus Christ," clearly seems to refer to John, not the angel (v. 2). The content may include more than the book of Revelation, but the additional words, "even to all that he saw," surely refer to visions and disclosures soon to follow. Verse 3 contains the first of seven beatitudes in Revelation, which John intended to be read publicly. The word "Blessed" means happy or fortunate and applies to both reader and hearers "who keep [heed] what is written therein." John's identification of his writing as a "prophecy" is another clue to the interpretation of the book. Although prophets were basically *forthtellers* of God's message, they often were *foretellers* or seers. Revelation includes both concepts. In the expression, "for the time is near," the word for time means opportune season, not the usual word for time from which we derive our term *chronology*. If chronology is meant here, the language is relative, like the term "last days," which refers to the indefinite period of time between the two advents of Christ (Acts 2:17).

Salutation (1:4-8)

John addressed himself "to the seven churches that are in Asia" (v. 4). Although the seven churches later are identified and respectively addressed with a letter, John likely included all the churches of the Roman province of Asia. In Jewish numerology, "seven" is the divine complete number, thus Peter's question to Jesus, "As many as seven times?" (Matt. 18:21). John gave the typical Christian greeting, "Grace to you and peace," with "grace" being an adaption of the Greek way of greeting and "peace" being the Jewish method. Grace has the connotation of favor, particularly divine favor, whereas peace basically means wholeness (physical, mental, and spiritual). The expression, "who is and who was and who is to come," refers to God the Father, whose covenant name (Yahweh) means "I am" or some other such equivalent (Ex. 3:14). He is the Eternal One, the God of the past, present, and future. The designation, "seven spirits who are before his throne," refers not to separate spiritual beings, but to completeness or fullness of spirit, thus the Holy Spirit. John then completed his trinitarian formula by adding, "and from Jesus Christ the faithful witness [martyr] the first-born of the dead, and the ruler of kings on earth" (v. 5a). Since Jairus' daughter, the son of the widow of Nain, and Lazarus were merely restored to physical life and later died again, Jesus' resurrection was uniquely different from theirs. Later John referred to Christ as "Lord of lords and King of kings" (17:14).

John dedicated his work to Christ as Redeemer (v. 5b). Christ not only "loves us," but he "has freed us from our sins by his blood." Although some manuscripts read "washed" instead of "freed" or loosed, the result is the same. The cross was the supreme example of divine love and the means of expiating or nullifying our sins (1 John 2:2). Christ also "made us a kingdom, priests to his God and Father" (v. 6). This statement echoes the teaching of 1 Peter 2:9: "But you are a chosen race, a royal priesthood, a holy nation, God's own people." Despite her high calling, Israel forfeited her privilege to be a priestly nation to the Gentiles. As Christians, we are the new Israel who are to represent God to others and others to God.

Verse 7 in part echoes the language of Zechariah 12:10 and reminds us of Acts 1:9-11. Although the return of Christ will be a happy occasion for believers, it will be a time of distress for unbelievers. The language strongly suggests an open, universally visible coming of Christ in which people of all historical ages will recognize him. The words, "every one who pierced him," may include Caiaphas and the Jewish leaders, Pilate and his soldiers, and, in a broader sense, the entire human race. Unlike the Roman emperor's limitations of both life and power, God is eternal and has all power (v. 8). "Alpha" and "Omega" are the first and last letters of the Greek alphabet, like our "A" to "Z." Thus, God is the eternal source of all things.

Call and Commission (1:9-11)

John claimed a fourfold relationship with his readers: (1) He was a Christian "brother"; he was also a (2) cosharer in "tribulation," (3) in "the kingdom," and (4) in "patient endurance" (v. 9a). This

fourfold relationship resulted from the fact that John and his readers
all were "in Christ," that is, had a vital faith union with Christ. John
further claimed that he was on the island of Patmos because of "the
word of God and the testimony of Jesus" (v. 9b). Since Patmos was
used as a Roman penal colony, John undoubtedly meant that he was
there as a prisoner. When John wrote that he was "in the Spirit on
the Lord's day," he probably meant that he was caught up in a
supernatural state of inspiration on Sunday, the first day of the week
(v. 10a). We may assume that the trumpet-like voice was that of
Christ because of the identity in verse 13 and the subsequent
description (v. 10b). The instruction to "Write what you see in a
book" (scroll) and to "send it to the seven churches" may well
include more than the forthcoming vision of the glorified Christ (v.
11). We may assume that the content of chapters 4—22 also went to
the seven churches, as well as to all the churches in Asia.

Vision of Christ Among His Churches (1:12-20)

When John turned "to see the voice," actually, the source of the
voice, he "saw seven golden lampstands," (v. 12), later identified as
"the seven churches" (v. 20). Next he saw "in the midst of the
lampstands one like a son of man" (v. 13a; Dan. 7:13). The following
description clearly identified this unique person as the glorified
Christ (vv. 13b-16). Although the description is similar to Christ's
appearance on the mount of transfiguration (Matt. 17:2), here we
have much greater detail. While we cannot be sure of the symbolism, perhaps the "long robe" pointed to his priestly function, and
the overall description, drawn particularly from Daniel and also
from other apocalyptic sources, depicted Christ in awe-inspiring
majesty. Since the "right hand" often referred to authority and
power, the fact that Christ held the seven stars in his right hand
suggests that he, not imperial Rome, had the final say concerning
what happened to the persecuted churches. The "sharp two-edged
sword" that issued from his mouth represented the word of God
(Heb. 4:12).

The fact that John "fell at his feet as though dead" stresses two
things: (1) John's feeling of inadequacy and inferiority and (2) the
deity and majesty of Christ (v. 17a). Isaiah had a similar experience
when he had a vision of God (Isa. 6:5), and likewise did Peter when
he caught a glimpse of Christ's deity (Luke 5:8). Despite John's fear,

his Lord assured him with both a touch and words (vv. 17b-18). The expression, "the first and the last," identifies the Son with the Father (v. 8); and the words, "I died, and behold I am alive for evermore," affirm Christ's death and resurrection. Since a key (or keys) was a symbol of authority (Matt. 16:19), the words, "I have the keys of Death and Hades," mean that Christ, not the Roman emperor or anyone else, has the ultimate authority over death and the spirit world beyond death. Hades (meaning "unseen") translates the Hebrew Sheol and refers to the unseen world of departed human spirits. Almost half the time Sheol means the grave in Old Testament usage (Gen. 42:38).

The glorified Christ instructed John to write three things: (1) "what you see," the present vision and probably those to follow; (2) "what is," which may mean both what currently is (for example, the condition of the churches) and what eternally is; and (3) "what is to take place hereafter" (literally, "after these things"), perhaps but not necessarily referring to events beyond the consummation of history (v. 19). Christ himself explained the symbolism of the "seven stars" and the "seven golden lampstands," the former being "angels of the seven churches" and the latter being the seven churches themselves (v. 20).

Four views of the seven angels include: (1) guardian angels of the churches; (2) the churches themselves personified; (3) messengers from the churches who visited John on Patmos; and (4) the ministers or pastors of the churches. Since Christ hardly would have addressed heavenly angels (messengers), since the second view seems unlikely, and since we have no knowledge of John having visitors from the seven churches, the most logical view is that the angels were the pastors (or at least prominent leaders) of the churches.

Letters to the Seven Churches (2:1 to 3:22)

All of the letters follow a similar pattern, with only slight variations: (1) commission to write; (2) distinguishing characteristics; (3) commendation; (4) reproof; (5) counsel; (6) encouragement; and (7) promise. Smyrna and Philadelphia receive no reproof, while Laodicea receives no commendation. The order of the letters logically follows the main roads connecting the seven cities. Just as environment today affects both the theology and ethics of churches, the same was true of these first-century churches.

Ephesus, the Spiritually Inconsistent Church (2:1-7)

The city of Ephesus was the largest city in the Roman province of Asia. Being a free city, it had self-rule granted by Rome. The most famous structure was the temple of the goddess Artemis, (Greek name) or Diana (Roman name). The magnificent temple was one of the seven wonders of the ancient world. Paul spent some three years there on his third missionary journey (Acts 19:1-20; 20:31). East met West there, and Ephesus became the center of gnosticism and the mystery religions. When John wrote, the emperor cult also was evidently strong in Ephesus. As verse 1 indicates, the letter came from the glorified Christ. The church received commendation for their "works," their "toil" (labor), and their "patient endurance" (steadfastness). Also, in their favor, they did not tolerate "evil men" and proved that certain self-proclaimed apostles were false. Whether these people included libertine Gnostics, Judaizers, or other heretical groups, we can only guess.

Verse 3 implies that the Ephesian Christians were both sound and faithful in doctrine. Yet the Lord registered a complaint against them by saying "that you have abandoned the love you had at first" (v. 4). While some limit their neglect to their love for Christ and the proclamation of the gospel, their problem seems to have been broader. Since love was to be the main distinctive of Jesus' disciples (John 13:35), perhaps they had largely ceased to demonstrate love toward one another and toward their opponents. The cure consisted in remembering their former state, repentance, and putting love into practice again (v. 5a). Otherwise, Christ would remove their "lampstand from its place" (v. 5b). This meant, of course, that their church would cease to exist, which, in fact, it eventually did.

A second commendation included their hatred of "the works of the Nicolaitans," which Christ also hated (v. 6). We should note that the hatred was directed toward their deeds, not the people themselves. Although the Nicolaitans perhaps were the same as the Balaamites (v. 14) or the followers of Jezebel (v. 20), one tradition holds that Nicolaus, one of the seven (presumably deacons), defected from the faith (Acts 6:5). Perhaps the Nicolaitans were libertine Gnostics.

The exhortation of verse 7 serves as both an encouragement and a warning. To anyone in the church who would heed his words, Christ promised: "To him who conquers I will grant to eat of the tree of life, which is in the paradise of God" (v. 7). The military figure of conquest is prevalent in Revelation. According to 12:11, believers overcame Satan "by the blood of the Lamb and by the word of their testimony, for they loved not their lives even unto death." We read in 1 John 5:4 that faith "is the victory that overcomes the world." Thus, the overcoming life includes faith in Christ and faithfulness in living godly lives as we proclaim his redemptive message even at the cost of our physical lives. The "paradise of God" reminds us of the garden of Eden and Adam's failure (Gen. 3:1-24). Those who "eat of the tree of life" are the ones partaking of the living bread (John 6:51).

Smyrna, the Spiritually Rich Church (2:8-11)

Smyrna (modern Izmir) was one of the chief cities of Asia. A port city, it had much commerce and was a city of culture. Although we have no knowledge of the founding of the church there, it is likely that converts from Paul's Ephesian ministry carried the gospel to Smyrna (Acts 19:10). History relates that Polycarp, the bishop (pastor) of the church, met a martyr's death there in AD 156. The description of the glorified Christ, like that concerning the letter to Ephesus, came from the vision of Christ in chapter 1.

He commended the church by saying: "I know your tribulation and your poverty (but you are rich) and the slander of those who say that they are Jews and are not, but are a synagogue of Satan" (v. 9). Because of persecution, which probably included economic sanctions, the church was materially poor. Yet at the same time it was spiritually rich. Condemnation of the Jews as "a synagogue of Satan" reminds us of Jesus' words to unbelieving Jews: "You are of your father the devil" (John 8:44). At first the Romans considered Christianity as a sect of Judaism, thus classified it as *religio licita* (legal religion). Apparently the Jews in Smyrna convinced the Roman authorities that Christianity was not a part of Judaism and should be classified officially as *religio illicita* (illegal religion) and thus exterminated according to Roman law.

The Lord encouraged the church not to fear their forthcoming suffering and imprisonment, which would test their faith during "ten days" of "tribulation" (v. 10*a*). Though we, of course, may take the "ten days" literally, the Jews sometimes used the number *ten* to symbolize human completion, probably because normal people have ten fingers and ten toes. Therefore, we suggest that the expression "ten days" refers to a definite, complete, but brief period of time. For their faithfulness "unto death," Christ promised them "the crown of life" (v. 10*b*). The word for *crown* means a victor's crown (wreath of greenery), given by Greeks and Romans to winners of athletic events. The expression "crown of life" means a life-kind of crown, consequently life itself. Although their persecution would be brief, apparently some of the members would be killed. In his earthly ministry, Jesus taught that his disciples should not fear them who can merely kill the body (Matt. 10:28). As indicated in the comments on the Ephesian letter, conquering begins with faith in Jesus as Savior and Lord. All who have such faith "shall not be hurt by the second death," that is, eternal separation from God (v. 11; 20:6,14).

Pergamum, the Spiritually Lax Church (2:12-17)

Pergamum was a prosperous city whose main distinction was its many pagan temples. Among these were temples to Zeus, the chief Greek god; Roma, the goddess of Rome; Aesculapius, the god of healing, with the familiar serpent symbol used by doctors today; and also temples to Dionysius and Athena. However, from the Christian viewpoint the most significant temple was the one dedicated to Augustus Caesar in 29 BC. Consequently, Pergamum was the center of the emperor cult in Asia. An official group known as the *concilia* enforced emperor worship not only locally but throughout the region. Almost certainly the reference to "Satan's throne" (v. 13*a*) alludes to the fact that Pergamum was the headquarters for the emperor cult.

The church had held fast Christ's name and had not denied his faith (v. 13*b*). According to biblical usage, one's name represented one's character or real self. For example, the name Jesus means Savior or Deliverer; Christ means Messiah or Anointed One. Perhaps the reference here is to Christ's lordship. The Christians at Smyrna were faithful to declare, "Jesus is Lord," and thus denied that Caesar was Lord. The expression "my faith" may mean Christ's faithfulness or perhaps their faith in him. Another possibility is that faith refers to the common body of Christian doctrine. At least one of their membership, identified only as "Antipas my witness, my faithful one," had died for his faith (v. 13c). However, despite their faithfulness, the Christians at Pergamum had been spiritually lax by tolerating an immoral group reminiscent of the sinning Israelites who followed the "teaching of Balaam" and whose sins included eating "food sacrificed to idols" and the practice of "immorality" or fornication (v. 14). Since gnosticism was widespread in Asia, quite likely the sinning group consisted of antinomian or libertine Gnostics who flaunted moral law. Because idolatry was considered spiritual adultery, we cannot be sure whether the immorality included idolatry, physical adultery, or both.

The Pergamum church, unlike the church at Ephesus, tolerated the Nicolaitans whose identity we have already noted (v. 15). The solution for the church at Pergamum was to "Repent"; otherwise, Christ said he would "war against them with the sword of my mouth" (v. 16). By this warning he probably meant that he would speak words of judgment against them.

Christ's promise "to him who conquers" was twofold: (1) a gift of "hidden manna" and (2) a "white stone" upon which was "a new name written . . . which no one knows except him who receives it" (v. 17). While the "hidden manna" may simply mean spiritual food, some believe the statement refers to the Jewish tradition that the ark of the covenant, containing a pot of manna, would be recovered in the messianic age. As for the meaning of the "white stone," we find that a white stone was used variously: (1) given to a person who had been tried in a court of law and acquitted; (2) given to a person who was freed from slavery; (3) presented to the winner of athletic events; (4) presented to a warrior returning from victory; (5) worn as a charm or amulet; and (6) related to the stones on the breastplate of the high priest. Possibly the white stone was a symbol of divine protection since calling one's name by the Roman government sometimes was a summons to death. However, the "new name" may refer to redeemed character. According to Old Testament usage, when a person had a change of character, he was given a new name, for example, Jacob to Israel (Gen. 32:28).

Thyatira, the Spiritually Divided Church (2:18-29)

As a city, Thyatira was a small but important trade center, noted for its production of purple dye. When Paul was at Philippi, he was instrumental in the conversion of Lydia, a woman from Thyatira and a "seller of purple goods" (Acts 16:14). Possibly Lydia later returned to Thyatira and started the church there. To the church, the risen Christ said: "I know your works, your love and faith and service and patient endurance, and that your latter works exceed the first" (v. 19).

For a church with such characteristics, one might assume that it would not have a negative side. The church was even making progress in its ministry to others. Yet in the church there was gross sin, which caused a spiritual cleavage. Although Jesus warned against being overly judgmental (Matt. 7:1-5), he also warned against being too uncritical (Matt. 7:6). Like the church at Corinth (1 Cor. 5:1-2), the church at Thyatira tolerated gross immorality. Whether the offending woman was actually named "Jezebel" or merely had a character like the long-dead wife of Ahab is uncertain. At least, she was immoral like Jezebel, called herself a "prophetess," and deceptively taught Christians "to practice immorality and to eat food sacrificed to idols" (v. 20). Because the word for woman and wife is the same, Jezebel possibly, but not probably, was the pastor's wife. Although Christ had given Jezebel an opportunity to repent of her immorality, she refused to do so (v. 21).

The language of verses 22-23 suggests idolatry (spiritual adultery) rather than physical adultery as the main sin of Jezebel and her followers, though both sins might have been involved. Whatever the case, Jezebel and her followers were bringing divine judgment upon themselves. The warning, "I will strike her children dead," seems more appropriately applied to Jezebel's converts than to her actual children. Christ's judgment upon Jezebel and her followers would serve as an example and a warning to other churches that he does not view sin lightly (v. 23). That Christ searches the "mind and heart" (literally, "kidneys and hearts") means that he knows our innermost emotions and thoughts. Although character determines conduct, conduct in turn reveals character. Consequently, judgment is always based on "works" (conduct).

Apparently Jezebel and her immoral followers felt that they were so spiritual that sins of the flesh did not matter. Perhaps they referred to their sins as "the deep things of Satan" and taunted their fellow church members with their alleged spiritual knowledge (v. 24). Their conduct suggests another case of libertine gnosticism.

Since Christ would not lay upon the spiritually faithful group "any other burden" (v. 24), perhaps their burden or obligation was twofold: (1) to expel Jezebel and her followers from the church and (2) to "hold fast what you have, until I come," that is, remain faithful (v. 25). The meaning of verses 26-27 is that the faithful believers will participate in the messianic reign (Ps. 2:8-9). Christ's gift of the "morning star" may refer to Christ himself as the Light of the world (v. 28). Otherwise, the star may mean the light of eternal salvation or some other similar idea.

Sardis, the Spiritually Dead Church (3:1-6)

Located on an easily guarded hill, Sardis nevertheless had fallen to enemies twice: first to Cyrus and the Persians, while rich King Croesus and his soldiers slept; and later to the Syrian king, Antiochus the Great, under similar circumstances. Although Sardis had declined from its former grandeur, it still was noted for its woolen and dyed goods industries, and among its several temples was the temple of Cybele, their patron goddess, who was associated with one of the prominent mystery religions. Along with Philadelphia, Sardis was destroyed by an earthquake in AD 17.

The church at Sardis received no commendation from the risen Christ. Rather, he said: "I know your works; you have the name of being alive, and you are dead" (v. 1). This scathing indictment indicates that the members were self-deceived into thinking they were spiritually mature. Perhaps they demonstrated a great deal of activity, which amounted to merely playing church. A common symptom of spiritual deadness is that the persons involved do not know that they have a problem (John 9:40-41).

However, every member of the church was not spiritually dead, as shown by the exhortation: "Awake, and strengthen what remains and is on the point of death" (v. 2). The imperative "Awake" more exactly is "Be watching." Perhaps there was an intentional play on the fact that the custodians of Sardis had been notably unwatchful in the past. If a church ever needed revival, the church at Sardis did. They also needed to remember what they had "received and heard," presumably the gospel, which they should retain; and they also needed to "repent," that is, have a radical change of mind resulting in a godly life-style (v. 3a). Possibly some of them had never experienced once-for-all repentance and faith, while others needed only to repent of occasional sin. The Lord then warned that if they were not vigilant he would come unexpectedly upon them "like a thief" (v. 3b; Matt. 24:42-44). Again the language seems to allude to the past history of Sardis when the city was captured because the guards slept.

Despite the spiritual inadequacy of the church as a whole, Christ said: "Yet you have still a few names in Sardis, people who have not soiled their garments; and they shall walk with me in white, for they are worthy" (v. 4). Soiled garments symbolize sinful lives. Paul used the language of putting off and on garments when he wrote: "Put off your old nature" and "put on the new nature" (Eph. 4:22,24). White garments clearly symbolize righteousness, perhaps victory also. The Sardis Christians were "worthy" because of what Christ did for them, not because of their own merit. The promise, "I will not blot his name out of the book of life," is complete assurance of salvation and does not imply that certain ones will have their names blotted out of the book of life (v. 5a). The concept of the book of life is common to both the Old Testament (Ex. 32:32-33; Ps. 69:28) and the New Testament (20:12). Since God has all knowledge, the book of life may be a figurative way of saying that God has known from eternity the names of all who will be saved. However, this fact need not imply that God chose certain ones to be saved and relegated the rest to eternal condemnation. Christ's second promise was: "I will confess his name before my Father and before his angels" (v. 5b). This statement reminds us of Jesus' words that he would confess before the Father the one who confesses Jesus before people (Matt. 10:32).

Philadelphia, the Spiritually Aware Church (3:7-13)

The name Philadelphia means "brother-lover" or "brotherly love." The city derived its name from its founder, Attalus II, who was surnamed Philadelphus because of his love for his brother Eumenes. Philadelphia was a border city and thus became a center for spreading Hellenism (Greek culture), including Greek language and customs. It was destroyed by an earthquake in AD 17. Afterward, many of the citizens preferred to live outside the city for fear of another earthquake. After being rebuilt by the emperor Tiberius, the city adopted the name "New Caesarea" in honor of Tiberius but later dropped it to assume the old name. The description of Christ as "the holy one" and "the true one" identified him with the covenant God of the Old Testament (v. 7*a*). Further description as the one "who has the key of David" means that he has authority as the Messiah. Possessing such authority, he has the full privilege to open or shut as he sees fit, with no one to hinder him (v. 7*b*). In the context, opening and closing seem to indicate opportunity or the lack of it.

Because of verse 8, Philadelphia has been called the church of the open door or the missionary church. Instead of spreading Greek culture, the church had a great opportunity for spreading the gospel. Despite opposition, no person or group would be able to cancel its opportunity. The expression, "you have but little power," suggests that the church was numerically weak; yet they were truly a faithful few (v. 8). Their greatest opposition obviously was from unbelieving Jews, described as "the synagogue of Satan" (v. 9*a*; 2:9). Because they refused to accept Christ and opposed his cause, these Jews were not true Jews, even as Jesus (John 8:39-40) and Paul (Rom. 2:25-29) had taught. The additional statement, that the Jews will bow before the Christians and recognize Christ's love for his church, is difficult to interpret (v. 9*b*). Since we have no indication that such recognition ever occurred in that day, the promise may await fulfillment in a final day of judgment.

Because the Philadelphia Christians had kept Christ's "word of patient endurance," he would keep them "from the hour of trial which is coming on the whole world, to try those who dwell upon the earth" (v. 10). Although futurists tend to identify this hour of trial with the great tribulation of the end time, it well may refer to final judgment of the wicked. Others tend to interpret this passage in terms of the distress associated with the persecution of Christians by Domitian. In New Testament usage, the Roman world was sometimes referred to as the "whole world" (Rom. 1:8, KJV). Likewise, the words, "I am coming soon" (v. 11*a*), must be interpreted in light of the truth "that with the Lord one day is as a thousand years, and a thousand years as one day" (2 Pet. 3:8). The exhortation, "hold fast what you have, so that no one may seize your crown," raises a serious problem (v. 11*b*). If the "crown" here is the same as the "crown of life" (2:10), as some maintain, does the passage mean that some Christians will lose their crowns, thus lose their salvation? The doctrines of preservation and perseverance are like two sides of the same coin. God preserves, and the believer perseveres. Only enduring faith is saving faith. The true Christian remains faithful to the end. Possibly "crown" here refers to the matter of spiritual rewards.

The spiritual conqueror is to become "a pillar in the temple of my God," never to "go out of it" (v. 12a). As the readers well knew, pillars were essential parts of temples and kept them from falling down. Unlike material pillars, believers are spiritual pillars in God's spiritual temple which he is in the process of building (Eph. 2:19-22). Against the possibility of losing one's salvation, the words, "never shall he go out of it," promise eternal security. Further assurance comes from the final promise "and I will write on him the name of my God, and the name of the city of my God, the new Jerusalem which comes down from my God out of heaven, and my own new name" (v. 12b). Whatever this promise means exactly, it certainly must refer to divine ownership and protection for every true believer. Perhaps there is an intentional contrast between the identifying mark of Christians and those who receive the mark of the beast (Rev. 13:16-18). Some see a contrast between the "new Jerusalem" and the name "New Caesarea," which Philadelphia had adopted. With reference to individuals, scriptural usage indicates that names stood for the essential person or character of the one bearing the name.

Laodicea, the Spiritually Indifferent Church (3:14-22)

As a city, Laodicea was known for its wealth, its manufacture of woolen goods, and its production of medical salve for the eyes. The wealth of the city was reflected in the attitude of the church. In contrast to Philadelphia, the church of the open door, Laodicea was the church of the closed door. In comparison with Smyrna, the materially poor but spiritually rich church, Laodicea was the materially rich but spiritually poor church. Noteworthy is the fact that Christ identified himself as "the Amen, the faithful and true witness, the beginning of God's creation" (v. 14). Since "Amen" means truly or surely, emphasis is on the truth and certainty of what Christ was saying. Although the expression, "the beginning of God's creation," may seem to imply that Christ was the first thing God created, such an interpretation is contrary not only to the teaching of Revelation, but also to that of the New Testament as a whole (John

1:1; Col. 1:15-16; Heb. 1:2). On the contrary, the words mean that Christ is the origin or source of all created things.

The complaint that the Laodicean church was "neither cold nor hot" shows that the church was spiritually indifferent or lukewarm (v. 15a). The plaintive "Would that you were cold or hot!" indicates the difficulty of inducing a positive response from people who are indifferent (v. 15b). Many pastors have learned from experience the difficulty of enlisting lukewarm Christians. Often the task of winning lost people seems easier than recruiting indifferent Christians. The lukewarm Laodicean church nauseated Christ, as revealed by his words: "So, because you are lukewarm, and neither cold nor hot, I will spew you out of my mouth" (v. 16).

Blinded by self-righteousness and self-deception, the members thought they were rich and prosperous, lacking nothing (v. 17a). From Christ's viewpoint, however, they were "wretched, pitiable, poor, blind, and naked" (v. 17b). The proposed cure, therefore, was to buy from Christ "gold refined by fire," "white garments," and "salve" for their eyes (v. 18). The play on words is quite obvious. The people needed real (spiritual) wealth, not material riches. "Gold refined by fire" means that all the dross had been burned out, just as persons need to have their sins purged. While the Laodiceans were famous for their excellent clothing, they needed "white garments," spiritual clothing, the imputed righteousness of Christ. Moreover, despite their manufacture of eye medicine, they needed spiritual "salve" for their blind eyes so they could really see.

Verse 19 reminds us of Hebrews 12:7-11. Because he is a loving Father, God disciplines his children, not arbitrarily or capriciously, but to help them develop spiritually. Thus, Christ appealed to the Laodiceans to "be zealous and repent." Then he uttered the touching, pleading invitation that has been repeated often in evangelistic efforts: "Behold, I stand at the door and knock; if any one hears my voice and opens the door, I will come in to him and eat with him, and he with me" (v. 20). Although the picture is that of a congregation behind closed doors, with Jesus on the outside knocking for admittance, the appeal must be understood individually. A well-known painting depicts no knob on the outside of the door, symbolizing the truth that Christ does not force himself on us but allows us the freedom of choice to accept or to reject him. The concept of eating together symbolizes intimate fellowship. Verse 21 indicates that "He who conquers" will share in Christ's spiritual reign, whether in heaven or on earth.

Although we see no merit in the view that the seven churches of Asia represent seven stages of church history, we are convinced that similar churches have existed throughout history and will continue to exist until the end of time. We further believe that individual churches may be like any one or more of these seven churches at different times in their history.

Vision of Heaven
4:1 to 5:14

God as Creator (4:1-11)

Through the letters to the seven churches of Asia, we have seen the conditions on earth. Now the scene shifts from earth to heaven. From the divine viewpoint, things look different.

God Enthroned (4:1-3)

The words "After this" (literally, "after these things") seem to refer not to chronology, but to a change in panorama (v. 1*a*). In the sequence of visions, the forthcoming vision is the second. John's new vision concerned an open door in heaven, and he received an invitation from a trumpet-like voice, saying, "Come up hither, and I will show you what must take place after this" or "after these things" (v. 1). The second use of "after this" may refer to the events beginning with 6:1. As was true of his earlier vision (1:10), John again was "in the Spirit," a supernatural state of inspiration (v. 2*a*).

The vision of God on his throne depicted his majesty and sovereignty and served the practical purpose of encouraging the persecuted and discouraged readers. The depiction of God by means of precious stones no doubt symbolized his majestic and awesome presence, but we can only guess about the symbolism of details. The three stones mentioned, the "jasper," "carnelian," (or sardius), and "emerald," apparently were the most precious known in that day. Perhaps the jasper was what we now call a diamond and symbolized God's holiness and transcendent majesty. The carnelian is a red stone and possibly referred to God's righteousness, resulting in judgment against sin. The rainbow "like an emerald" (a green stone) represented God's promise (Gen. 9:12-17), signifying life and hope. All three stones were on the breastpiece of the high priest (Ex. 28:15-21) and also in the foundation of the New Jerusalem (21:19-20). Interestingly, the emerald-colored rainbow was a complete circle around the throne, not a semicircle as seen from the earth's vantage point.

Twenty-four Elders (4:4)

Identification of the "twenty-four elders" in verse 4 seems best resolved by using Jewish numerology. Twelve was the number for organized religion or worship, thus twelve tribes of Israel and twelve apostles. Moreover, from David's time (1 Chron. 24:1-19) the priesthood was divided into twenty-four courses, representing twenty-four sections of the country. The number two symbolized strength, certainty, and witness (Gen. 41:32; Deut. 17:6). Consequently, the twenty-four elders seem to represent the totality of redeemed humanity. Their "white garments" and "golden crowns" (victors' crowns) suggest righteousness, spiritual purity, and victory.

Seven Spirits of God (4:5)

The "flashes of lightning, and voices and peals of thunder" from the throne remind us of the covenant at Sinai (Ex. 19:16-24) and apparently signified God's holiness, majesty, righteousness, and wrath toward sin (v. 5a). Since seven was the number for divine fullness or completion, the "seven spirits of God" probably referred not to angelic beings but to the Holy Spirit (v. 5b).

Four Living Creatures (4:6-8)

The "sea of glass, like crystal" before the throne may refer to God's transparent holiness, but it also seems to indicate his transcendence with reference to sinful mankind (v. 6a). Later, in the heavenly state, "the sea was no more" (21:1). John next saw "four living creatures, full of eyes in front and behind" (v. 6b). These creatures were not beasts, though two of them are described in beastlike terms. The fullness of eyesight possibly means great spiritual vision. According to a more specific description we read: "the first living creature like a lion, the second living creature like an ox, the third living creature with the face of a man, and the fourth living creature like a flying eagle" (v. 7).

John likely borrowed the description from Ezekiel 1:10. Who or what were these living creatures? One suggestion is that they were cherubim, which respectively symbolized the following: (1) the lion, strength; (2) the ox, service; (3) the man, intelligence; and (4) the eagle, swiftness. Perhaps more meaningful is the view that the four creatures represented all created things according to the natural division of that time: (1) the lion, wild beasts; (2) the ox, domestic animals; (3) man, mankind; and (4) the eagle, birds. The additional description that they had "six wings" (v. 8a) is reminiscent of Isaiah's version of the seraphim (Isa. 6:2-4). While we must guess about the details, the overall meaning comes through clearly: The entire creation praises its Creator. Consequently, the living creatures "day and night . . . never cease to sing, 'Holy, holy, holy, is the Lord God Almighty, who was and is and is to come!'" (v. 8b). The word "holy" means set apart and designates the moral transcendence of God, who is altogether removed from that which is sinful. God also is "Almighty," that is, omnipotent, having all power, the Eternal One.

Universal Worship of God (4:9-11)

Following the lead of the living creatures, the twenty-four elders joined them in praising God (vv. 9-10a). In humble devotion and adoration, the elders "cast their crowns before the throne, singing, 'Worthy art thou, our Lord and God, to receive glory and honor and power, for thou didst create all things, and by thy will they existed and were created'" (vv. 10b-11). Contrary to the view that heaven will be mainly a family reunion according to earthly ties, this passage suggests that in heaven God's family willingly and joyfully will spend eternity singing praises to him.

Christ as Redeemer (5:1-12)

John's heavenly vision had a shift in focus from the first to the second person of the holy Trinity.

The Lord of History (5:1-5)

John recorded: "And I saw in the right hand of him who was seated on the throne a scroll written within and on the back, sealed with seven seals" (v. 1). The fact that the scroll had writing on both sides indicates the completeness of its contents. The expression, "sealed with seven seals," means that it was fully or completely sealed. Although sealing sometimes denoted protection and ownership, here the central idea is that its message was concealed. However, the symbol of ownership may show that the message is God's.

As the scene unfolded, John saw a "strong angel" who loudly proclaimed, "Who is worthy to open the scroll and break its seals?" (v. 2). However, "no one in heaven or on earth or under the earth was able to open the scroll or to look into it" (v. 3). The phrase "under the earth" is typical Jewish terminology and refers to Sheol or Hades, the realm of the dead. Quite possibly, here it means the grave, which is a common meaning of Sheol. Distressed because no one could be found worthy to open the scroll, John wept (v. 4). Then one of the elders consoled him by saying, "Weep not; lo, the Lion of the tribe of Judah, the Root of David, has conquered, so that he can open the scroll and its seven seals" (v. 5). The language, of course, is clearly messianic.

The Slain Lamb (5:6-10)

Next John "saw a Lamb standing, as though it had been slain, with seven horns and with seven eyes, which are the seven spirits of God sent out into all the earth" (v. 6). Paradoxically, Christ is both a "Lion" (v. 5) and a "Lamb." As a lion, he is King and Judge. As a lamb, he is the eternal sacrifice for the sins of mankind (7:14). Another aspect of the paradox is the "wrath of the Lamb" (6:16). Since animals used their horns to fight, horns symbolized power, and "seven horns" denote complete power. The Lamb's "seven eyes" mean complete spiritual vision and really are "seven spirits of God," that is, the Holy Spirit. Just as Jesus identified himself with the Father (John 14:9), he also identified himself with the Holy Spirit (John 14:16-18). The slain, risen, glorified Lamb was the only one worthy to take the scroll from the Father's hand (v. 7).

After he had taken the scroll, "the four living creatures and the twenty-four elders fell down before the Lamb, each holding a harp, and with golden bowls full of incense, which are the prayers of the saints" (v. 8). The same kind of praise and adoration that was given to the Father now was given to the Son. The "new song" of verses 9-10 was a song of redemption wrought by Christ's shed blood. The verb translated "didst ransom" means "purchased," as the *goel* or redeemer kinsman of the Old Testament purchased his less fortunate kinsman out of slavery (Lev. 25:47-48). Reference to "every tribe and tongue and people and nation" shows the universal nature of Christ's redemption. The song of redemption reiterated the fact that believers are a kingdom of priests, thus having the privilege of representing themselves and others to God. Some interpret the statement "and they shall reign on earth" to be positive proof that Christians will participate with Christ in a literal reign on earth. Yet others insist that the reign on earth is spiritual in nature and is presently taking place.

The Worthy Lamb (5:11-12)

Joining the living creatures and the elders were "myriads of myriads and thousands of thousands" of angels in a mighty, heavenly choir, "saying with a loud voice, 'Worthy is the Lamb who was slain, to receive power and wealth and wisdom and might and honor and glory and blessing!'" Since a "myriad" is ten thousand, the writer meant to convey the idea of countless thousands of angels. This impressive scene served to emphasize the incomparable love and greatness of our wonderful Savior.

Father and Son Worshiped (5:13-14)

In a climactic act of worship, "every creature in heaven and on earth and under the earth and in the sea, and all therein," joined together in a vast, universal throng to praise both God the Father and God the Son. This thrilling, awe-inspiring passage in effect says what Paul did when he wrote "that at the name of Jesus every knee should bow, in heaven and on earth and under the earth, and every tongue confess that Jesus Christ is Lord, to the glory of God the Father" (Phil. 2:10-11).

The Seven Seals
6:1 to 8:5

This section shows the message of the seven-sealed scroll to be the events of history under the sovereignty of Christ. However, we should not interpret his sovereignty in terms of extreme predestination. Both divine sovereignty and human freedom are real. Yet when the final curtain has been rung down on the drama of human history, we may be certain that God's purpose will have been accomplished. Although God, of course, has no problem understanding his own will, because of our extremely limited perspective, we need to think of God's will in a threefold way: (1) his intentional will; (2) his permissive or circumstantial will; and (3) his ultimate will. Since the scroll in the Lamb's hand concerned history, the question is: What aspect of history was intended? The idealist or philosophy of history believer says all of history. The preterist says the history of the downfall of the ancient Roman empire. The continuous-historicist says the immediately unfolding history of the church. The futurist says the portion of history just before the end time. Even though all four views have merit, this writer believes that Revelation's primary interest is with first-century Rome, whose history spilled over into subsequent history.

The First Seal—White Horse (6:1-2)

To expedite history, "the Lamb opened one of the seven seals," after which John heard one of the four living creatures say in a thunderous voice, "Come!" (v. 1). Because some Greek manuscripts read, "Come and see," there is a question as to whether John, the rider of the horse, or the horse itself was addressed. Although the correct meaning does not affect the overall interpretation, the Revised Standard Version follows what seems to be the preferred reading. Accordingly, the command was a signal for the horseman to ride dramatically across the stage. Perhaps the figure of the four horsemen was derived from Zechariah (1:8-11; 6:1-8). Since Christ is the rider of the white horse in 19:11-16, some interpreters conclude that Christ is the rider of the white horse here also. Others say it represents the gospel, which God uses to accomplish his purpose in history. As noted earlier, white may symbolize either righteousness (moral purity) or victory or both. Perhaps because of the problem of symbolism, at least one writer has said the rider was the Antichrist, who imitated righteousness. Another problem stems from the fact that the rider of the white horse in chapter 19 had a sharp two-edged sword for his weapon. Here the weapon is a bow, which suits neither Christ nor the gospel. Thus, the rider of the white horse seems to represent military conquest, which God uses throughout history to accomplish his purpose. Here, then, the symbolism of white is limited to the idea of conquest. This interpretation agrees best with the description, "and he went out conquering and to conquer" (v. 2).

The Second Seal—Red Horse (6:3-4)

There seems to be unanimous agreement that the red horse represents war. Perhaps the chief weakness in our interpretation of the white horse as military conquest is that it seems to overlap the meaning of the second horse. Despite the similarity, however, war and bloodshed necessarily accompany conquest—thus a need for two different horses. The rider of the red horse "was given a great sword," symbolizing great slaughter. Although God does not inspire the evil that promotes war, in his sovereignty he uses war to accomplish his will. For example, he used the Assyrians and the Babylonians to chastise Israel and Judah. Later he used the Persians to restore the Jews to their homeland.

The Third Seal—Black Horse (6:5-6)

The black horse depicts the scarcity, famine, and inflated prices that accompany war. The "balance" seems to indicate rationing. In the first century, a "denarius" was a day's wage for common labor, and a "quart of wheat" was the daily ration for a Roman soldier. Thus, prices were so high that an entire day's labor was required for daily sustenance of one person. No doubt many poor people got by on less than a quart of wheat. Otherwise, they ate barley, which was three quarts for a denarius. The expression, "do not harm oil and wine!" may represent the sarcastic attitude of the conquerors, showing that oil and wine were available, but that the poor could not afford them.

The Fourth Seal—Pale Horse (6:7-8)

The meaning of the pale horse is clear since "its rider's name was Death, and Hades followed him." As noted previously, Hades (Hebrew, Sheol) means the unseen, spirit world, the realm of the dead, the grave. The antecedent of "they" in the statement, "and they were given power over a fourth of the earth," may refer exclusively to Death and Hades, but the additional words, "to kill with sword and with famine and with pestilence and by wild beasts of the earth," seem to include the first three horses and their riders. A "fourth of the earth" indicates a sizable but limited destruction. Reference to destruction "by wild beasts" may refer to those who died in Roman arenas. Eventually the Roman empire, which lived by conquest, would fall by conquest, as Jesus said to Peter, "for all who take the sword will perish by the sword" (Matt. 26:52).

The Fifth Seal—Martyrs (6:9-11)

Assuming that the first four seals related to militarism in general and Roman militarism in particular, which boomeranged on Rome in terms of judgment, the fifth seal gives the main reason for divine retribution against Rome, the blood of the martyrs. Accordingly, John "saw under the altar the souls of those who had been slain for the word of God and for the witness they had borne." We should note that "souls" here are synonymous with spirits (selves). Yet, in either case, we are not to assume that persons are complete as disembodied souls or spirits. The Bible depicts human beings as a unity of body and soul (spirit), thus the necessity for a resurrection body. Against the view that the martyrs were vengeful and bloodthirsty, they only wanted divine justice to be vindicated. Their cry was like the inaudible cry of Abel's shed blood (Gen. 4:10). Their cry implied a moral necessity for judgment. John records that the martyrs "were each given a white robe" (symbolic of moral purity and victory), and they were "told to rest a little longer, until the number of their fellow servants and their brethren should be complete, who were to be killed as they themselves had been." The exhortation to patience seems to indicate that Roman persecution had not yet run its full course.

The Sixth Seal—Terror of the Wicked (6:12-17)

Although the principle of sin and retribution sometimes seems incredibly slow in its unfolding, retribution does finally come. In a terrifying description, painted in vivid apocalyptic language, the opening of the sixth seal reveals the terror of the wicked as they faced the reality of reaping the full consequences of their sins. Those who interpret the apocalyptic language literally misunderstand the nature of apocalyptic writing. For example, some stars are larger than the earth and could hardly fall "as the fig tree sheds its winter fruit when shaken by a gale" (v. 13). The cataclysmic events depicted are similar to the cosmic woes used to describe the coming of the day of the Lord (Joel 2:30-31). Men who were proud, arrogant, and supposedly bold and brave, now acted the role of cowards, which at heart they were all the time. Bullies become suddenly timid when confronted with a person or a situation they cannot handle. Thus, as John saw the matter from God's viewpoint, wicked men called "to the mountains and rocks, 'Fall on us and hide us from the face of him who is seated on the throne, and from the wrath of the Lamb'" (v. 16). According to the writer of Hebrews, "It is a fearful thing to fall into the hands of the living God" (Heb. 10:31). To reject God's love eventually means to receive his wrath (God's continuing opposition to evil).

Is the judgment depicted here limited to the destruction of imperial Rome? Is it a preview of final judgment? On the other hand, does it depict the consequences of sin during any and every era of history? According to futurists, it refers to the punishment of wicked men in the end time, prior to final judgment and perhaps associated with the battle of Armageddon. Partially because of the expression, "great day of their wrath," it seems to be the picture of final judgment.

A Parenthesis: Preservation of the Saints (7:1-17)

Just as Israel was protected from the plagues against Egypt, true believers will be protected from the judgment to befall wicked, unregenerate people as described by the opening of the sixth seal. Chapter 7 answers the question closing chapter 6: "who can stand before it?" that is, the divine wrath of the sixth seal.

Sealing of the 144,000 (7:1-8)

Introductory to this parenthetical section, John "saw four angels standing at the four corners of the earth, holding back the four winds of the earth, that no wind might blow on earth or sea or against any tree" (v. 1). Since four was the cosmic number, the "four angels," "four corners," and "four winds" all naturally relate to the earth. However, the language here does not necessarily mean that John thought the earth was flat. In the context, the four winds clearly symbolize divine retribution, which temporarily was being restrained, as shown by the appearance of "another angel" who instructed the four angels to refrain from inflicting damage against nature until God's servants were sealed (vv. 2-3). The sealing denoted both divine ownership and protection. Apparently, however, the saints were to be delivered not *from* tribulation but *through* it. Prohibition against hurting the earth, the sea, and the trees (v. 3) refers to the first four trumpets, which were to be woes upon nature. The reference to God's servants being sealed on their "foreheads" is no doubt to be contrasted with the reference to those who had the mark of the beast on their foreheads (13:16).

The identity of the 144,000 is a highly disputed issue. Futurists tend to identify them with a quota of Jews who will be saved in the end time, quite possibly an exact number of 12,000 from each tribe, during the great tribulation. Others claim the 144,000 represent, whether figuratively or literally, the quota of martyrs. However, the passage says nothing about their deaths. Another view holds that the 144,000 consist of both Christian Jews and Gentiles who constitute spiritual Israel, the true church here on earth. Among other problems, the question of tribal names is prominent. First of all, the several lists of the tribes of Israel vary considerably. Usually when Joseph's son Manasseh is mentioned, so is his son Ephraim, whereas Joseph's name is omitted. In such a list, another tribe must be omitted (usually Levi or Dan) to total twelve tribes. Here, however, we note the inclusion of both Joseph and Manasseh and the omission of Ephraim and Dan. Irenaeus, an early church father, claimed on the basis of the noncanonical Testament of Dan that the Antichrist would come from the tribe of Dan. However, regardless of one's theory of the Antichrist, a Jewish antichrist seems highly improbable.

According to Jewish numerology, twelve symbolizes organized religion, and ten is the number for human completion. Three is the divine or infinite number (for example, the divine Trinity). Simple mathematics tells us that 1,000 is the result of multiplying $10 \times 10 \times 10$, and that 144 is the square of 12. The resultant symbolism shows that the 144,000 is the total number of the saints, not to be taken literally as Jehovah's Witnesses do, but figuratively to represent a large, perfect, or complete, number. The context indicates the true church on earth.

The Innumerable Multitude (7:9-17)

Next John saw "a great multitude which no man could number, from every nation, from all tribes and peoples and tongues, standing before the throne and before the Lamb, clothed in white robes, with palm branches in their hands" (v. 9). Although some identify these believers with the 144,000 above, this view is unlikely. For example, no sealing is involved, since these saints already are in heaven and need no sealing. Others insist that the great multitude consists of Gentile Christians in contrast to the 144,000 who are Jewish Christians. Another view holds that they are all martyrs, not in the primary sense of witnesses, but in the secondary sense of witnesses who died for their faith. It seems best to see this multitude as consisting of both Jewish and Gentile Christians in heaven; thus, they are the *church triumphant*. Their "white robes" symbolize righteousness and victory. The "palm branches" may derive from the Feast of Tabernacles celebration and denote joy and deliverance. The praising of God described in verses 10-12 is similar to the heavenly scene in chapters 4 and 5. According to verse 13, one of the elders asked John the identity and origin of those "clothed in white robes." When John replied that his questioner knew their identity, the elder said, "These are they who have come out of the great tribulation; they have washed their robes and made them white in the blood of the Lamb" (v. 14).

The term "great tribulation" has about the same number of interpretations as there are views of Revelation as a whole. Preterists say the term describes the persecution of Domitian. Idealists (philosophy of historicists) identify the great tribulation with the earthly experience of all the children of God. Futurists claim it refers to tribulation connected with the end time. If the saints of God being described are truly the totality of believers in heaven (the church triumphant), the great tribulation, accordingly, must describe the trials and tribulations that all of God's children endure during their earthly pilgrimage. This view, however, allows for specific manifestations of intense tribulation. Verses 15-17, in poetic imagery, depict the bliss that the great multitude enjoys in their heavenly state. Life for them is not static. They serve God day and night. In turn, God "will shelter them with his presence" (v. 15). Additionally, "They shall hunger no more, neither thirst any more"; nor will they suffer from the sun or "scorching heat" (v. 16). The Lamb "will be their shepherd, and he will guide them to springs of living water; and God will wipe away every tear from their eyes" (v. 17).

The Seventh Seal—Altar of Incense (8:1-5)

Despite the problems and trials on earth, God's church has ultimate security, both the members on earth and those in heaven. Moreover, God's servants now have the assurance that wicked people will receive their just dues. Although there has been a parenthesis to disclose the preservation of the saints, before divine retribution begins by the opening of the seventh seal, John recorded that "there was silence in heaven for about half an hour" (v. 1). Perhaps the brief silence signified delayed judgment or was merely a device for dramatic effect, a suspense builder. Another possibility is that the delay allowed time for the prayers of the saints to be heard. Next John "saw the seven angels who stand before God," to whom were given seven trumpets (v. 2). In the meantime, "another angel came and stood at the altar with a golden censer; and he was given much incense to mingle with the prayers of all the saints upon the golden altar before the throne" (v. 3). The altar of incense indicates that God will hear the prayers of his people. Moreover, he will vindicate them by judging evil as indicated by the "peals of thunder, voices, flashes of lightning, and an earthquake" when the angel took the censer, filled it with fire from the altar, and threw it on the earth (v. 5). This dramatic action was a foreboding of what would soon happen when the trumpets sounded.

The Seven Trumpets
8:6 to 11:19

As we shall note, the first four trumpets were plagues upon nature according to the natural divisions of that day: (1) land, (2) sea, (3) fresh waters, and (4) heavenly bodies. Whether the seven seals, seven trumpets, and seven bowls should be interpreted as occurring simultaneously or consecutively is debatable. From the standpoint of the drama, they are consecutive. However, from the standpoint of history, they very well may be simultaneous.

The First Trumpet: Natural Disasters (8:6-7)

When "The first angel blew his trumpet . . . there followed hail and fire, mixed with blood, which fell on the earth" (v. 7a). Except for the mention of blood, this plague is very similar to the seventh plague against Egypt (Ex. 9:24), and the blood is reminiscent of the first Egyptian plague. Seemingly the fire caused the most damage since "a third of the earth was burnt up," as well as "a third of the trees" and "all green grass" (v. 7b). Instead of taking a third to be an exact amount, we interpret it to mean a large part. We should note that all of these first four plagues were against nature and affected people only indirectly. The fact that the destruction was incomplete may mean that even in judgment God extends mercy, as was characteristic with his dealing with Israel. Perhaps the central message of the first trumpet is that God uses land disasters to punish and to warn the wicked. Of course, this would be true of all ages of history. However, natural disasters, like the eruption of Mount Vesuvius in AD 79, were instrumental in the fall of imperial Rome.

The Second Trumpet: Maritime Disasters (8:8-9)

When "The second angel blew his trumpet . . . something like a great mountain, burning with fire, was thrown into the sea." The result was that "a third of the sea became blood, a third of the living creatures in the sea died, and a third of the ships were destroyed." The second trumpet suggests that God uses maritime disasters to punish and to warn the wicked.

The Third Trumpet: Floods and Epidemics (8:10-11)

When the third angel sounded his trumpet, "a great star fell from heaven, blazing like a torch, and it fell on a third of the rivers and on the fountains of water." According to John, the star's name was "Wormwood," an extremely bitter-tasting wood, which made a third of the fresh water bitter and poisonous, resulting in the death of many. Instead of resorting to a great deal of imagination in attempting to decipher symbols, this writer prefers to believe that John depicted floods and epidemics resulting from drinking polluted water caused by floods. Accordingly, the third trumpet teaches that God uses floods and epidemics to punish and to warn the wicked.

The Fourth Trumpet: Heavenly Bodies (8:12)

The blowing of the fourth trumpet adversely affected a third of the sun, a third of the moon, and a third of the stars. Resultantly, "a third of their light was darkened; a third of the day was kept from shining, and likewise a third of the night." Perhaps, like the first three trumpets, this one also reveals that God uses the heavenly bodies (for example, eclipses and falling meteorites) to punish and to warn the wicked.

A Parenthesis: Eagle Vision (8:13)

The eagle vision comprises another interlude, perhaps for dramatic effect. Because it was a bird of prey, the eagle sometimes was considered an ill omen. Yet even God is depicted as an eagle (Ex. 19:4). However, the present context indicates that this particular eagle had bad news for bad people. The three utterances of "woe" stress the fact that the final three trumpets will be three woes "to those who dwell on the earth." Consequently, the intermission serves to emphasize the impending judgments.

The Fifth Trumpet (First Woe): Satanic Destruction (9:1-12)

The fifth trumpet becomes the first woe (v. 1). John "saw a star fallen from heaven to earth, and he was given the key of the shaft of the bottomless pit" (v. 1). Views of the symbolism of the star vary greatly, including the following: (1) Satan himself; (2) an angelic being in control of the forthcoming plague; (3) a star personified; (4) a fallen angelic being other than Satan. According to the details, the most obvious view is that the star symbolizes Satan. The fact that the "key" (authority) was given to him suggests that any authority Satan possesses is derived authority, according to the permissive will of God. In 1:18, we noted that Christ has the key to Death and Hades. The smoke from the bottomless pit and the subsequent darkness it caused apparently symbolized the moral darkness caused by Satan. Perhaps taking his cue from the locust plague against Egypt (Ex. 10:12-19), John used the symbolism of a locust plague to depict the devastation wrought by sin. Although ordinary locusts do not harm people directly, these locusts were instructed specifically not "to harm the grass of the earth or any green growth or any tree, but only those of mankind who have not the seal of God upon their foreheads" (v. 4). Just as Satan's authority was delegated, the locusts "were allowed" not to kill evil people, but "to torture them for five months," the usual length of a locust plague, but here

probably used symbolically of a considerable but limited time (v. 5).
Whether the torment is physical or the pain of an evil conscience,
the description reveals the consequences of unforgiven sin. Verse 6
depicts the frustrations of wicked men as they seek death but are
unable to find it. The apocalyptic language in verses 7-10, used to
describe the appearance and the destructive power of the locusts,
defies exact interpretation. To conclude that they allude to modern
military equipment (like tanks or helicopters) seems altogether
unwarranted. So does the historicist view that the language describes the Muhammadan conquests. The most convincing interpretation of the creatures' tails having the power to hurt (v. 10) is
that they symbolize the Parthian cavalry who shot one arrow when
they charged, then turned around on their mounts to shoot another
arrow as they retreated. However, there is danger in seeking a
specific identity.

Although ordinary locusts do not have a king (Prov. 30:27), these
demonic locusts "have as king over them the angel of the bottomless
pit; his name in Hebrew is Abaddon, and in Greek he is called
Apollyon" (v. 11). Both names mean Destroyer and seem to refer to
Satan. Despite our inability to understand John's symbolic language
with certainty, the overall message comes through. Under the
symbolism of a locust plague, John has described the powers and
influences of hell, the devastation wrought by sin, and the moral
corruption of the Roman empire that the author knew so well.
Perhaps John also meant to teach that God uses Satan and his
demonic forces to punish and to warn.

The Sixth Trumpet (Second Woe): Demonic Cavalry (9:13-21)

If the last passage was difficult to understand, this one is equally if
not more difficult. John heard a heavenly voice, perhaps God's,
command the sixth angel with a trumpet: "Release the four angels
who are bound at the great river Euphrates" (vv. 13-14). The
significance of the Euphrates was at least twofold: (1) it was the
northern boundary of the Promised Land (Gen. 15:18), and (2) the
Romans viewed it as the eastern border of the Roman empire. From
the viewpoint of Greek and Roman culture, peoples who lived
beyond the Euphrates were barbarians. These peoples included the
warlike, uncouth Parthians, who served as a sort of thornlike irritant

in the side of arrogant, mighty Rome. According to verse 15, the four loosed angels had been held in waiting for the exact time in God's calendar "to kill a third of mankind." As noted before, a third probably designated a large but limited portion. The tremendous cavalry consisted of "twice ten thousand times ten thousand" (200,000,000) troops (v. 16). While some believe John symbolically referred to the Parthian cavalry, others interpret the passage literally to depict a huge army, perhaps composed of both Russians and Chinese, in the end time. Still others believe that they refer to demonic beings or to a second phase of the Muhammadan conquests. The horses are similar but different from the creatures described under the symbol of a locust plague. Both had tails that inflicted damage. However, these horses have lionlike heads that spew smoke and sulphur from their mouths, whereas the others had humanlike faces and lionlike teeth.

Does this dreadful cavalry symbolize the downfall of imperial Rome or does it depict the devastation wrought upon all people by sin and rebellion? On the other hand, does this vision teach that God uses war with all its horrors to punish and to warn the wicked? Whatever the case, the survivors did not repent of their works but continued to worship demons and lifeless idols (v. 20). Neither "did they repent of their murders or their sorceries or their immorality or their thefts" (v. 21). Contrary to the view that all punishment is corrective, this passage implies that punishment is both penal and corrective. Otherwise, God would have to let the incorrigible wicked go free.

A Parenthesis: Strong Angel with a Small Book (10:1-11)

Between the sixth and seventh trumpets (the second and third woes), there are two parenthetical passages. According to verse 1, John saw a "mighty angel coming down from heaven, wrapped in a cloud, with a rainbow over his head, and his face was like the sun, and his legs like pillars of fire." Who was this magnificent angel? There is no merit in the view that the angel symbolized Christ. The huge angel "had a little scroll open in his hand," and he placed "his right foot on the sea, and his left foot on the land" (v. 2). Since the sea and land included the entire world, the message in the scroll was universal.

Next the giant angel cried out with a lionlike voice, which drew a response from the "seven thunders," not otherwise identified (vv. 3-4a). As John was about to write, a voice from heaven commanded: "Seal up what the seven thunders have said, and do not write it down" (v. 4b). Here sealing means to prevent the disclosure of the message uttered by the seven thunders. The significance of the sealing is not readily apparent. Possible reasons include: (1) no more warning to be given; (2) information too sacred to be divulged; (3) cancellation of additional plagues. Dramatically, the huge angel raised "his right hand to heaven" and made a solemn oath by God himself, the Creator of all things, "that there should be no more delay, but that in the days of the trumpet call to be sounded by the seventh angel, the mystery of God, as he announced to his servants the prophets, should be fulfilled" (vv. 5-7). Since the word for "delay" is *chronos,* usually translated time, the clause may be translated "that time shall be no longer." However, the end of historical time does not seem to be the intended meaning. Rather, God was about to reveal his purpose, which included protection of God's people and further punishment of his enemies. The "mystery of God" may refer to his redemptive purpose, revealed partially through his prophets, and fully through his Son (v. 7). Although the gospel is good news to those who accept it, paradoxically, it becomes bad news to those who reject it. To reject God's love means inevitably to receive his wrath.

Next the heavenly voice instructed John to go to the giant angel and take the scroll from his hand (v. 8). Having done as he was instructed, John then was told: "Take it and eat; it will be bitter to your stomach, but sweet as honey to your mouth" (v. 9). Having obeyed the unusual command, John discovered that the result of eating the scroll was exactly as the heavenly voice had said. (See Ezek. 2:9 to 3:3.) Apparently eating the scroll meant thoroughly digesting or understanding its message. The message was sweet because it was God's word and also because it contained grace and mercy for the receptive. On the contrary, it was bitter because it contained judgment for the unreceptive. Even though the content of the scroll may not be certainly known, it seems to refer to the forthcoming disclosures in the Book of Revelation. Such an interpretation best fits the instructions given to John: "You must again prophesy about many peoples and nations and tongues and kings" (v. 11).

A Parenthesis: The Two Witnesses (11:1-14)

Prior to the sounding of the seventh trumpet (third woe), John was given the special task of measuring "the temple of God and the altar and those who worship there" (v. 1). The word for *temple* means "sanctuary" and usually designated the holy of holies. Since the Jewish Temple had been destroyed by Titus and his Roman forces in AD 70, John could not have meant the magnificent Temple built by Herod the Great. Futurists insist that a new Jewish temple will be built in the end time. According to Paul, however, the community of believers, the church, is the temple of God (Eph. 2:19-22). Measuring obviously means measuring or marking out for divine protection. Accordingly, the church will be protected, not from physical harm, but from ultimate, spiritual harm during the forthcoming judgment against the enemies of God.

The "court outside the temple," that is, the court of Gentiles, was not to receive divine protection, "for it is given over to the nations, and they will trample over the holy city for forty-two months" (v. 2). If the temple refers to God's children (spiritual Israel), the court of Gentiles must refer to unbelievers, whether Jews or Gentiles, who will not have God's protection. The "forty-two months" are otherwise described as "one thousand two hundred and sixty days" (v. 3), "a time, and times, and half a time" (12:14). Instead of taking the view that interprets this 3½-year period literally, or the view that converts 1260 days into 1260 years, this writer believes that it refers to an indefinite period of time. Apparently the term "holy city" refers to Jerusalem.

The identity of the "two witnesses" (v. 3) is perhaps the most debated issue in Revelation. Suggestions include: Moses and Elijah; Enoch and Elijah; Christ and John the Baptist; Jewish and Gentile Christians; Saint Francis and Saint Dominic; the law and the prophets; the prophetic order and the apostolic order; the true church and the preacher of truth; a strong gospel witness; Christian martyrs; the whole preaching activity of the early Roman period; the preached word and the administration of the sacraments.

According to verse 4, "These are the two olive trees and the two lampstands which stand before the Lord of the earth" (Zech. 4:1-14). During the indefinite time of their prophecy, the two witnesses will enjoy divine protection. Just as God's word in Jeremiah's mouth was a fire that devoured unfaithful Israelites (Jer.

5:14), fire from the mouths of the two witnesses is to devour those who would harm them (v. 5). We may assume that the fire was God's word spoken by them in judgment. The account here also may derive from the story of Elijah, when fire came down from heaven and destroyed the men King Ahaziah sent to arrest the prophet (2 Kings 1:9-16). The description of the prophets' power to withhold rain and to turn water to blood and "smite the earth with every plague" seems clearly to refer to Elijah and Moses (v. 6). These two Old Testament saints apparently symbolized the law and the prophets, just as they did on the mount of transfiguration (Matt. 17:1-8). Jesus himself said, "For all the prophets and the law prophesied until John," and Jesus went on to identify John with Elijah (Matt. 11:13-14).

The central message of the law and the prophets pointed to Jesus and thus merged into the gospel, which triumphed greatly until it was hindered by the extreme persecution of Domitian. Consequently, the death of the witnesses (the gospel) at the hands of the "beast" (Domitian) meant a temporary barrier for the church. Yet the severe persecution of Domitian could not destroy the gospel witness. Reference to the witnesses' bodies lying "in the street of the great city which is allegorically called Sodom and Egypt, where their Lord was crucified," surely designates Jerusalem (v. 8). Mention of Sodom reminds us of excessive sinfulness and divine rejection, just as Egypt was symbolic of the oppression of God's people. Perhaps Jerusalem herself was symbolic of the abstract worldly city of wickedness in contrast to the heavenly city of righteousness, the new Jerusalem.

Although the futurists hold that the two witnesses (perhaps Moses and Elijah) will be actual persons to testify in the end time, the apocalyptic nature of the language seems best interpreted as we have suggested. Accordingly, the viewing of "their dead bodies" (which were refused burial), as well as the rejoicing of their enemies, also must be interpreted figuratively (vv. 9-10). The "three days and a half" probably refer to a relatively short period of time. The resurrection of the two witnesses (v. 11) is reminiscent of Ezekiel's vision of the valley of dry bones, which symbolized the restoration of the Jews to their homeland (Ezek. 37:1-14). In addition, the resurrection and ascension of Jesus may be in the background, since the two witnesses "went up to heaven in a cloud" (v. 12). The gospel triumphed over Roman persecution and survived

in a mighty display of divine power. Following the ascension of the
two witnesses, there occurred "a great earthquake, and a tenth of
the city fell; seven thousand people were killed in the earthquake,
and the rest were terrified and gave glory to the God of heaven"
(v. 13). Although this difficult passage has been interpreted to mean
a limited destruction of Jerusalem and the subsequent conversion of
Israel in the end time, we see the event as a limited and relative
judgment against wicked people who were forced to recognize
God's sovereignty, but who did not trust him for the forgiveness of
sins. It seems unlikely that this passage ever can be identified with a
particular historical event.

The Seventh Trumpet (Third Woe): Heavenly Victory (11:15-19)

In John's dramatic presentation, chapter 10:1 to 11:13 has been an
interlude between the sixth and seventh trumpets (second and third
woes). Now John resumed his trumpet account as "the seventh angel
blew his trumpet, and there were loud voices in heaven, saying,
'The kingdom of the world has become the kingdom of our Lord and
of his Christ, and he shall reign for ever and ever'" (v. 15). Perhaps
more than coincidence is involved in the fact that silence followed
the opening of the seventh seal (8:1), whereas "loud voices" followed
the blowing of the seventh trumpet. The loud voices suggest the
heavenly excitement concerning God's triumph over evil. The
seventh trumpet closes the first major section of Revelation and
serves as a transition to the second and final section.

In a general sense, chapters 1—11 depict the earthly conflict
between the forces of good and evil, whereas chapters 12—22 depict the heavenly conflict. Although God's sovereignty is eternal, he
chose to create human beings with a freedom of choice, thus
permitting them to trust God or to rebel against him. Yet God will
not tolerate mankind's rebellion forever. The "kingdom [reign] of the
world" stands in opposition to the "kingdom [reign] of our Lord and
of his Christ." God asserted his sovereignty (kingdom) in a direct
and personal way through the earthly ministry of Jesus. Later Christ
will bring the kingdom to completion and submit it to his Heavenly
Father (1 Cor. 15:28).

In the passage before us, the consummation of the kingdom is announced as if it has already occurred, thus stressing the fact of its certainty. John depicted the twenty-four elders as falling on their faces, worshiping God, and thanking God that he has taken his "great power and begun to reign" (v. 17). Perhaps alluding to Psalm 2, verse 18 refers to the nations in their rebellion against God, final punishment, and the rewarding of God's children. The expression, "for destroying the destroyers of the earth," implies the moral principle of sin and retribution. Thus, the destroyers finally destroyed themselves. "Then God's temple in heaven was opened, and the ark of his covenant was seen within his temple; and there were flashes of lightning, voices, peals of thunder, an earthquake, and heavy hail" (v. 19). This language, of course, is symbolic. Both the Temple and the ark of the covenant were symbols of God's presence. Later John wrote that the heavenly city has no temple (21:22). Why should there be a symbol when God himself is present? The ark of the covenant also symbolized that God will keep his covenant with his people. On the other hand, the dramatic natural phenomena symbolized God's judgment upon the wicked. Both salvation and judgment are inevitable in a truly moral universe.

Visions Concerning the Great Conflict
12:1 to 14:20

The Woman, Child, and Dragon (12:1-17)

The first scene in the great cosmic conflict between God's forces and Satan's forces centers around God's incarnation in the person of Jesus Christ, the seed of woman who bruised the head of the serpent (Gen. 3:15).

Woman and Child Versus Dragon (12:1-6)

John related that "a great portent [sign] appeared in heaven, a woman clothed with the sun, with the moon under her feet, and on her head a crown of twelve stars" (v. 1). The first impression is that the radiant woman refers to national Israel, but she later evolved into spiritual Israel, the church. Thus, the "twelve stars" may be interpreted as both the twelve tribes and the twelve apostles. The fact that the woman was "with child" suggests that Israel produced the Messiah (v. 2). To identify the woman as the virgin Mary does not do justice to the message.

Following the sign of the woman and child, "another portent appeared in heaven; behold, a great red dragon, with seven heads and ten horns, and seven diadems upon his heads" (v. 3). Verse 9 identifies the dragon as "that ancient serpent, who is called the Devil and Satan, the deceiver of the whole world." The "seven heads" likely symbolize great wisdom, the "ten horns" great power over mankind, and the "seven diadems" great authority or kingship. Elsewhere Satan is described as "the ruler of this world" (John 12:31) and "the prince of the power of the air" (Eph. 2:2). The dragon's ability to sweep down "a third of the stars of heaven, and cast them to the earth" shows his great destructive ability (v. 4a). Moreover, his departure from heaven to earth may reflect the idea that from now on his activities will be limited to the earth.

Next "the dragon stood before the woman who was about to bear a child, that he might devour her child when she brought it forth" (v. 4b). Satan's efforts to destroy Christ included: (1) Herod's destruction of the children of Bethlehem; (2) Jesus' temptations; (3) Judas' betrayal; and (4) the cross. Paradoxically, however, Satan met his defeat at the cross (John 12:31), fulfilling God's word to the serpent in the Garden of Eden (Gen. 3:15). Verse 5, alluding to the messianic promise of Psalm 2, states that the woman "brought forth a male child, one who is to rule all the nations with a rod of iron." The additional information, that "her child was caught up to God and to his throne," clearly refers to Christ's ascension. Subsequently, "the woman fled into the wilderness, where she has a place prepared by God, in which to be nourished for one thousand two hundred and sixty days" (v. 6). Although the language reminds us of Israel's wilderness wanderings, it particularly seems to refer to Roman persecution of the church for a lengthy but indefinite period of time, the same period of time mentioned in chapter 11:2-3 concerning the trampling of the holy city by the nations and the prophesying of the two witnesses. Alternate interpretations of verse 5 identify the "male child" with Constantine, the martyrs of the coming persecution, and the rapture of the living saints together with the resurrection of dead saints. However, none of these seems to merit serious consideration.

Dragon Cast from Heaven (12:7-12)

We must be careful not to take this passage literally. Otherwise, we merely compound the problem. According to the account, "Now war arose in heaven, Michael and his angels fighting against the dragon; and the dragon and his angels fought, but they were defeated and there was no longer any place for them in heaven" (vv. 7-8). If this account is in chronological sequence, the expulsion of Satan from heaven is yet future, not past, according to the popular view as depicted by John Milton in *Paradise Lost*. Moreover, we must remember that the Book of Job depicts Satan as traveling back and forth from earth to heaven (Job 1:6-12; 2:1-7). Michael, an angel (messenger) of God, is mentioned several times in the Bible (Dan. 10:13,21; 12:1; Jude 9). According to Jude, Michael is an archangel or chief angel. The apocryphal Book of Enoch names Michael as one of the seven archangels. Ultimately, however, Christ, not Michael, defeated Satan at the cross (Luke 10:18).

Although verse 9 depicts "the great dragon," identified as "that ancient serpent . . . the Devil and Satan, the deceiver of the whole world," as being cast down to earth together with his angels, we must be cautious about identifying this fall as a specific historical event. Yet the defeat of Satan signaled a cry of heavenly victory as John heard "a loud voice in heaven, saying, 'Now the salvation and the power and the kingdom of our God and the authority of his Christ have come, for the accuser of our brethren has been thrown down, who accuses them day and night before our God'" (v. 10). As in Job, this passage indicates Satan's access to God. The term "Devil" means accuser or slanderer, whereas "Satan" means adversary or opponent. According to biblical usage, there is only one devil—but many demons, who serve as the devil's agents. Significantly, the heavenly voice continued to say, "And they have conquered him by the blood of the Lamb and by the word of their testimony, for they loved not their lives even unto death" (v. 11). The expression, "word of their testimony," probably refers to the Christian confession, "Jesus is Lord," in contrast with those who said, "Caesar is Lord." During Domitian's reign, to confess the lordship of Christ often meant death.

Verse 12 consists of both joyfulness and warning, joyfulness for heaven and its occupants, and warning for "earth and sea, for the devil has come down to you in great wrath, because he knows that his time is short!" Thus, the already persecuted Christians were to prepare themselves for another assault by Satan. The brevity of Satan's time may mean thousands of years according to God's calendar (2 Peter 3:8).

Woman Persecuted by Dragon (12:13-17)

Frustrated by his defeat, the dragon "pursued the woman who had borne the male child" (v. 13). Even though the woman, originally national Israel, has now become spiritual Israel, the church, we are not to conclude that the church produced Christ. Despite Domitian's effort to destroy the church, God came to the church's rescue. No doubt "the two wings of the great eagle" (v. 14a) symbolize the protective care of God (Ex. 19:4; Deut. 32:11; Isa. 40:31). As noted earlier, "a time, and times, and half a time" is identical with 42 months or 1260 days. It apparently is symbolic of a somewhat lengthy but indefinite period of time, quite possibly the same as a "thousand years" (Rev. 20:2). According to verse 15, the serpent attempted to overwhelm the woman with a flood. However, the earth aided the woman "and swallowed the river which the dragon had poured from his mouth" (v. 16). The water may refer to persecution or perhaps to false doctrines, which always have tended to destroy the church from within. Whatever the exact significance of the flood, Satan renewed his persecution efforts against the church by making "war on the rest of her offspring, on those who keep the commandments of God and bear testimony to Jesus" (v. 17).

Because of the reading, "And he stood on the sand of the sea," the Revised Standard Version translators transposed the sentence from 13:1 and added it to verse 17 of chapter 12. Other Greek manuscripts read, "And I stood on the sand of the sea." The Revised Standard Version seems not only to represent better manuscript evidence, but also seems to conform better to the context. Accordingly, Satan stood on the sand of the sea looking for someone to carry out his purpose to persecute the church.

The Dragon's Helpers (13:1-18)

The First Beast (13:1-10)

John recorded that he "saw a beast rising out of the sea, with ten horns and seven heads, with ten diadems upon its horns and a blasphemous name upon its heads" (v. 1). The "sea" was a common metaphor for masses of people or nations (perhaps in turmoil), as shown in 17:15. In apocalyptic literature, beasts often symbolized nations or empires (Dan. 7:3-8). Contrary to the view that the sea beast refers to the Roman Catholic Church (historicist) or an end-time antichrist (futurist), this writer believes that it represents imperial Rome as John knew it. Symbolically, "ten horns" refer to complete human or worldly power, "seven heads" to great wisdom (pretending to be divine wisdom), and "ten diadems" to complete human or worldly power as expressed through political rule. The expression "a blasphemous name" seems to refer to the egocentric claim to deity by the Roman emperors. For example, the Roman senate honored Julius Caesar, Augustus, Claudius, Vespasian, and Titus with divine rank following their deaths. The name *Augustus* is a Latin title of majesty, which, when translated into Greek as *Sebastos*, takes on the connotation of deity. Caligula ordered his statue to be placed in the Jewish Temple, and Domitian required his attendants to kiss his feet and all of his subjects annually to pledge allegiance by saying, "Caesar is Lord and God."

John's description of the beast (v. 2a), as a composite of three other beasts, corresponds closely with Daniel's account of four beasts, which likewise came up out of the sea (Dan. 7:2-7). Daniel's beasts are in chronological order: lion (Babylonia), bear (Media), leopard (Persia), and the fourth kingdom (the Greek Seleucid rulers, particularly the wicked Antiochus Epiphanes). Later Jewish interpreters identified the fourth kingdom with Rome. John's beast was "like a leopard" (Greece), with feet "like a bear's" (Medo-Persia), and with a "mouth . . . like a lion's" (Babylonia). Thus, John reversed the chronological sequence in his description and depicted Rome as a ferocious composite of the three kingdoms that immediately preceded it. Apparently this beast is identical to the beast of 11:7. Like the dragon, the sea beast had ten horns and seven heads (17:3); but whereas the dragon had seven diadems (kingly crowns) on his seven heads, the beast had ten diadems on his ten horns. John seemingly varied his symbols. For example, the "seven heads" are identified as both "seven mountains" and "seven kings" (17:9-10) and the "ten horns" as "ten kings" (17:12).

Since the dragon was looking for someone to carry out his program of persecuting the church, he "gave his power and his throne and great authority" to the beast (v. 2b). If the seven heads refer to seven Roman emperors (17:10), the beast's head that survived a mortal wound seems to allude to the Nero *redivivus* legend, which may be a parody of Christ's death and resurrection (v. 3). According to the legend, Nero did not die permanently when he committed suicide in AD 68, and supposedly he later would return, perhaps leading an army of Parthians. Since both Nero and Domitian persecuted Christians, John apparently used the legend to his own advantage by describing Domitian as Nero all over again. John, of course, did not believe the legend was true, but his readers would readily grasp his message. Verse 4 stresses the grim reality of emperor worship, which actually was devil worship, as all forms of idolatry are (1 Cor. 10:20). The Roman empire was so extensive and powerful that her faithful admirers said: "Who is like the beast, and who can fight against it?"

The arrogant beast uttered "haughty and blasphemous words, and it was allowed to exercise authority for forty-two months" (v. 5), the same length of time the nations trampled the Holy City and God's two witnesses prophesied (11:2-3). Verse 6 further emphasizes the blasphemous actions of the Roman emperors, and Domitian in particular. The beast (Roman empire), under God's permissive will, "was allowed to make war on the saints and to conquer them" (v. 7a). Although some, who argue for an end-time antichrist and a reactivated Roman empire, insist that ancient Rome did not exercise authority "over every tribe and people and tongue and nation" (v. 7b), Paul wrote that the faith of the Roman Christians had been proclaimed "in all the world" (Rom. 1:8). The additional statement, "and all who dwell on earth will worship it, every one whose name has not been written before the foundation of the world in the book of life of the Lamb that was slain" (v. 8), does not necessarily refer to more than the extent of the Roman world. John, of course, could have used hyperbole (see John 21:25). For example, Paul wrote that the gospel "has been preached to every creature under heaven" (Col. 1:23). The main point John intended to make was that emperor worship was so widespread and accepted that only faithful Christians refused to participate. Verse 10 is both a call to nonviolent resistance and to faithful endurance on the part of Christians. The thought seems to be derived from Jeremiah 15:2 and Jesus' words to Peter on the occasion of Jesus' arrest (Matt. 26:52). The words "if any one slays with the sword, with the sword must he be slain" represent a general principle which militant Rome one day would experience.

The Second Beast (13:11-18)

From the viewpoint of Asian Christians, the first beast was foreign, "out of the sea." In contrast, the second beast was native, "out of the earth" (v. 11a). Consequently, if the first beast was imperial Rome, personified by Domitian, then the second beast was provincial Rome, represented by the *concilia* or organization for enforcing emperor worship. The fact that the second beast "had two horns like a lamb and spoke like a dragon," indicates two things: (1) false religion and (2) satanic power. Since a lamb was a religious symbol, the second beast was related to emperor worship. Because animals fight with their horns, to John horns symbolized power. Moreover, the fact that the second beast "spoke like a dragon," shows that it exercised the power of Satan as expressed through the first beast.

Some interpreters believe that the second beast represented pagan religions because they assisted the emperor by opposing Christians. Futurists tend to identify the first beast as an end-time political dictator who has the backing of the second beast, the head of a worldwide church organization. Some historicists believe that the first beast was the Roman Catholic Church, headed by the Pope, whereas the second beast was the hierarchy supporting the Pope in his effort to put down all dissidents, as in the Inquisition during the Middle Ages. However, we may question whether any other view than imperial and provincial Rome would have made sense to the persecuted Christians of John's day. According to verse 12, the second beast "exercises all the authority of the first beast . . . and makes the earth and its inhabitants worship the first beast, whose mortal wound was healed." This description supports the view we have suggested. The final clause seems to refer to the Nero *redivivus* legend.

The "great signs" performed by the second beast, though they deceived superstitious people who knew not God, probably were bogus miracles, which in reality were merely clever magicians' tricks (v. 13). The act of "making fire come down from heaven" perhaps was a trick designed to imitate Elijah's miracle (2 Kings 1:10). Furthermore, the feat of giving life to the beast's image, including speech, no doubt was fakery, possibly involving ventriloquism (v. 15). According to verse 16, the second beast, exercising the authority of the first, used economic sanctions to force all people, "both small and great, both rich and poor, both free and slave," to carry out the will of the first beast. In order that no one could escape from the emperor's design, provincial Rome controlled all trade by requiring all buyers and sellers to have an identifying mark of the beast on "the right hand or the forehead" (vv. 16-17a). The mark was "the name of the beast or the number of its name" (v. 17b). John then proceeded to challenge his readers to apply their wisdom and understanding by calculating "the number of the beast, for it is a human number, its number is six hundred and sixty-six" (v. 18). Some manuscripts read "six hundred and sixteen."

Throughout Christian history, interpreters have struggled with the number of the beast. Before the invention of Arabic numbers, many peoples used the letters of their alphabets for numbering purposes. Most of us are familiar with roman numerals, but we may know nothing at all about Greek and Hebrew numerals, also derived from their respective alphabets. Irenaeus in the second century discovered that the Greek *lateinos* (or Latinus) added up to 666. Consequently, Irenaeus identified the Latin church as the beast. Later someone discovered that Nero in Greek form, but with Hebrew letters, equals 666, whereas Nero in Latin form, but with Hebrew letters, adds up to 616. But why should a Roman emperor's name be converted into alphabets other than his native Latin? Reportedly, the Pope's crown is inscribed with the Latin phrase *vicarius filii dei*, which means "in place of the son of God." The roman numerical value of this title is 666. By assigning arbitrary values to letters of the English alphabet, later efforts have come up with the names of Hitler and others.

All such efforts are intriguing and perhaps amusing, but in the long run they are futile. The most reasonable conjecture is that John again used typical Jewish numerology. Since seven was the divine perfect number, six was the imperfect number. A perfect number of sixes, three sixes, expressed infinite evil. Accordingly, the beast (from the sea) was the opposite of all that is divine and perfect. Put another way, the beast was the cruelest, most ungodly person imaginable.

Although we have avoided calling the beast *the Antichrist,* he at least was *an antichrist* since all who are opposed to Christ are in some sense antichrists. Yet John, who only in his first two Epistles used the term *antichrist,* never once referred to either beast as an antichrist. Jesus used the term "desolating sacrilege" (Matt. 24:15), also translated "abomination of desolation" (KJV), and Paul wrote of the "man of lawlessness" or "son of perdition" (2 Thess. 2:3) to describe an unnamed antichristian person. Whether Jesus and Paul referred to the same person is debatable, and whether John's first beast is to be identified with the person designated by either Jesus or Paul (or both) is open to question. However, if we assume that all three meant one particular person, the evidence seems to point to Domitian as the Antichrist. Yet this conclusion does not rule out the possibility, if not probability, of an end-time antichrist. As long as sinful people oppose God's will and his supreme self-revelation in the person of Jesus Christ, there will be antichrists.

The Lamb and His People (14:1-5)

In the cosmic drama, John now takes his readers to a scene that is the opposite of the one they had just witnessed. Although power and victory seemed to be on the side of Satan as he worked through the two beasts, real power and victory are on the side of the Lamb and his forces. John saw "on Mount Zion . . . the Lamb, and with him a hundred and forty-four thousand who had his name and his Father's name written on their foreheads" (v. 1). The mark perhaps signified ownership, protection, and safety. Earlier we saw the 144,000 in chapter 7:4-8. In contrast to the followers of the beast, the 144,000 had the names of the Lamb and his Father on their foreheads. Verses 2-3 portray the notion of beauty, majesty, awe, and mystery as the 144,000 "sing a new song before the throne and before the four living creatures and before the elders" (v. 3). Apparently, the "new song" was the same new song of 5:9-10, the song of redemption. The fact that the scene is heavenly does not necessarily mean that the 144,000, depicted as alive in 7:4-8, were now dead. Rather, this grandiose view suggests that the 144,000 comprise the totality of the redeemed of all time. Because only the redeemed can understand the meaning of redemption, only the 144,000 "could learn that song."

John's description of the redeemed as "these who have not defiled themselves with women, for they are chaste" (v. 4a), may allude to the Old Testament concept that soldiers should abstain from sexual relations prior to going into battle (1 Sam. 21:5). Symbolically, such abstinence applies to God's spiritual soldiers, although in no sense does this passage support the doctrine of a celibate priesthood or celibacy within marriage. Since the Bible depicts idolatry as spiritual adultery, abstinence from idolatry may be the meaning here. Of course, John could have referred to sexual immorality. Yet we must use great caution about imposing a literal interpretation. Otherwise, no females would be included among the redeemed. The 144,000 "follow the Lamb wherever he goes" and "have been redeemed from mankind as first fruits for God and the Lamb" (v. 4b). Following the Lamb indicates discipleship. Ordinarily, the term "first fruits" refers to the first bundles of grain presented to God at the Feasts of Passover (barley harvest) and Pentecost (wheat harvest), with the expectation that the full harvest would follow. Here, first fruits may or may not symbolize that other believers will be added. At any rate, the 144,000 are a holy offering to God. Verse 5 represents the language of sacrifice. Just as sacrificial animals were without blemish, these saints were free of falsehood, "for they are spotless."

Series of Angel Visions (14:6-13)

Angel with Eternal Gospel (14:6-7)

We have seen the dragon (Satan) and his puppets, the two beasts, representing the forces of evil. Opposed to them are the Lamb and his army of redeemed followers. However, instead of an immediate battle, John wrote that he "saw another angel flying in midheaven, with an eternal gospel to proclaim to those who dwell on earth, to every nation and tribe and tongue and people" (v. 6). So, instead of immediate judgment upon the wicked, we learn that God's nature is to give unregenerate people another opportunity to repent. This is another example of divine judgment tempered with mercy. Because "gospel" does not have a definite article before it, some insist that the message here was the gospel (good news) to believers in the sense that God would soon judge the wicked. However, such an interpretation robs the term *gospel* of its usual meaning by violating the context. Consequently, the "eternal gospel" is still the good news of Christ's death and resurrection on behalf of sinners. Moreover, the appeal was universal, as indicated by the words, "to every nation and tribe and tongue and people." John urged them to heed the invitation to "Fear God and give him glory . . . and worship him who made heaven and earth, the sea and the fountains of water" (v. 7). We glorify God by bearing spiritual fruit as Jesus' disciples (John 15:8). The expression, "for the hour of his judgment has come," may refer to final judgment, to God's judgment against Rome, or to both. To illustrate, the downfall of Rome was symbolic of the final defeat of all evil.

Angel Announcing Babylon's Downfall (14:8)

Just as Jezebel became the symbol of evil womanhood, ancient Babylon became the symbol of an evil city. Yet there can be little doubt that John had ancient Rome in mind. Likewise, Peter also meant Rome when he wrote, "She who is at Babylon . . . sends you greetings" (1 Pet. 5:13). Because the fall of Rome was as sure as the moral law of sowing and reaping is constant, the second angel announced Rome's fall as if it already had happened, for Rome's eventual fall was certain.

Angel Announcing Punishment and Reward (14:9-13)

The message of the third angel contained both a threat and a promise. Those who identified themselves with the beast faced a dreadful fate. Using Old Testament language (Isa. 51:17; Jer. 25:15), John affirmed that every follower of the beast would "drink the wine of God's wrath, poured unmixed into the cup of his anger" (v. 10a). Although the Scriptures depict God's wrath as a calm, fixed opposition to evil, the word rendered "anger" indicates a more volatile expression of God's disfavor toward evil, somewhat like an outburst of temper. While some interpreters tend to play down God's punishment of sin, we must remember that his wrath is the opposite side of the coin from his love. Otherwise, there could not be a moral universe. Despite attempts to remove God from the moral law of sowing and reaping (Gal. 6:7), God was the one responsible for creating a moral universe, including the principle in question.

According to the further description of divine wrath, every follower of the beast "shall be tormented with fire and sulphur in the presence of the holy angels and in the presence of the Lamb" (v. 10b). The picture here is reminiscent of the destruction of Sodom and Gomorrah (Gen. 19:24-28). Contrary to the view that such punishment is cruel, inhuman, and sub-Christian, we must note several things. First, evil is so bad that it deserves punishment. Second, the language is symbolic, though it depicts a grim and painful reality. Third, since God is just, no one will receive more or less punishment than he deserves. Finally, God does not punish sinners eternally for finite sins. Rather, the experience of hell is such that rebellious sinners will have no inclination to repent, just as we noted earlier (9:20-21). On the contrary, sinners in hell will be on a never-ending treadmill of sin and punishment. The moral law of sowing and reaping, in the negative sense, will be a permanent reality. As in the story of the rich man and Lazarus (Luke 16:19-31), one aspect of punishment will be the realization of lost opportunity. Yet, simultaneously, unbelievers will be engrossed in self-pity and self-justification. In contrast with the righteous (14:13), the wicked have "no rest, day or night" (v. 11), age without end.

The warning to the wicked was "a call for the endurance of the saints, those who keep the commandments of God and the faith of Jesus" (v. 12). If some of the Christians were tempted to spare themselves immediate suffering by worshiping the emperor, John's words served as both warning and encouragement. By "the faith of Jesus," John could have meant faith in Jesus or Jesus' faithfulness unto death. Because of the definite article, John also could have meant Christian faithfulness to the body of truth related to the person and ministry of Jesus. Verse 13 serves the much needed purpose of assuring severely persecuted Christians that those who die for their faith will have a commensurate heavenly reward. The heavenly state, though not static, will involve rest from earthly labors.

Vision of the Harvest Judgment (14:14-20)

John's harvest vision includes two kinds of harvest: grain and grapes. Both are symbols of judgment. Interpreters, however, disagree sharply about the details. Some insist that the grain harvest concerns only believers and that the grape harvest concerns only unbelievers. Yet in Jesus' parable of the weeds or tares (Matt. 13:24-30,36-43), the harvest included both the "sons of the kingdom" and the "sons of the evil one" (Matt. 13:38). John probably derived the concept of a dual harvest of grain and grapes from Joel 3:12-13. Reference to a "white cloud" may symbolize purity and victory, and in the Scriptures clouds are often associated with deity. Jesus described "the Son of man coming on the clouds of heaven" (Matt. 24:30). Moreover, Luke recorded that at Christ's ascension "a cloud took him out of their sight" (Acts 1:9).

Although some interpret the phrase, "one like a son of man," to designate an angel, John probably referred to Christ, who had "a sharp sickle in his hand" (v. 14). While some object to an angel commanding Christ to reap the harvest, others point out that the angel "came out of the temple," apparently meaning that the angel bore God's message (v. 15). Those who hold the latter view point out that Jesus said only the Father knew the time of his return (Matt. 24:36). Moreover, Jesus once said that he always did that which was pleasing to the Father (John 8:29). The added description that "the harvest of the earth is fully ripe" suggests that the gospel had been widely proclaimed, and wicked people had been given an opportunity to repent (v. 15).

The fact that an angel, not Christ, harvested the grapes does not prove that the grain harvest symbolized only believers, while the grape harvest signified only unbelievers. Because the Father has given all judgment to the Son (John 5:22), the angel who reaped the grapes is Christ's agent (vv. 17-19). According to verse 20, "the wine press was trodden outside the city, and blood flowed from the wine press, as high as a horse's bridle, for one thousand six hundred stadia" (about 200 miles). We may assume that "city" refers to Jerusalem, although we should not press a literal interpretation. The Jews traditionally taught that God would judge the nations (Gentiles) from Jerusalem (Zech. 14:1-4).

While some see safety for Christians within the city, others see safety "outside the city." For example, the author of Hebrews urged

Christians to go "outside the camp" because Jesus suffered "outside
the gate" (Heb. 13:12-13). According to the latter view, the blood
perhaps had a dual meaning: (1) the blood of the Christian martyrs
and (2) the blood of their enemies, the former being the ultimate
cause of the latter. However, mention of "the wrath of God" supports
the view that only the blood of the wicked was meant. The
description of the pool of blood of the wicked being two hundred
miles long and coming up to a horse's bridle symbolizes the infinite
punishment of the wicked. The wicked had caused the shedding of
the Christians' blood, but at the judgment a reversal of the situation
would occur.

In the context, the twofold harvest seems to refer to judgment
against ancient Rome. Also, it seems to be identical with the battle
of Armageddon (16:16), which in turn seems to symbolize final
judgment. One problem of reconciling these references concerns
chronology. Although we may prefer a chronological sequence of
events, John's series of judgments may be simultaneous rather than
consecutive. For example, Jesus seemingly taught only one basic
judgment (Matt. 25:46; John 5:28-29).

Seven Bowls of Divine Wrath
15:1 to 16:21

Introductory: Prelude to Judgment (15:1-8)

Chapter 15 is introductory to the seven bowls of wrath in chapter
16. We saw in chapters 12 and 13 the expulsion of the dragon (Satan)
from heaven, his attempt to kill the child (Jesus), his vengeful
persecution of the woman (the church), and his recruitment of the
sea beast (imperial Rome) and the land beast (provincial Rome) to
continue the persecution of the church. Then in chapter 14, we saw
the Lamb (Christ) and the 144,000 (the totality of the redeemed)
standing in opposition to Satan and his forces. Also, we noted in
chapter 14 a twofold harvest (symbolic of both redemption and
judgment), which served as a sort of preview of the ultimate

separation of the righteous from the wicked. Chapter 15, as we noted, is somewhat parallel with Israel's deliverance from Egypt through the Red Sea.

Seven Angels with the Seven Plagues (15:1)

Just as John earlier saw a portent (sign) in heaven (12:1), again he "saw another portent in heaven, great and wonderful, seven angels, with seven plagues, which are the last, for with them the wrath of God is ended" (v. 1). The practical purpose of this new portent was to assure the persecuted saints on earth to be faithful even to death, because they would share in God's ultimate victory over evil. The basic meaning of *plague* is a blow or stroke, or a wound or bruise resulting from a blow or stroke. Since the forthcoming "seven plagues" are called "the last," and since their expedition meant that "the wrath of God is ended" (was completed), why are there other punishments mentioned in chapters 19 and 20? Rather than resort to the subtlety that the latter punishments are not actually "plagues," perhaps the solution lies in the fact that John used terms and concepts with two or more meanings. We already have seen that the glorious woman (12:1) evolved from national Israel to spiritual Israel (the church). Moreover, the 144,000 of 7:4 seemingly became the church triumphant in 14:1 and consequently blended into the innumerable multitude of 7:9. Therefore, we conclude that from the temporal viewpoint, the seven plagues (bowls of wrath) were divine judgments against imperial Rome. Yet, from the viewpoint of eternity, they represent God's judgment against all of sinful, unrepentant humanity.

Heavenly Victory Celebration (15:2-4)

Apparently the "sea of glass" (v. 2) was the same sea of glass John described earlier (4:6). As in the former reference, the sea of glass still symbolized God's transcendence and served as a barrier between God and sinful mankind. However, here in the heavenly state, "those who had conquered the beast and its image and the number of its name" were no longer separated from God. The words "mingled with fire" seem to point to the approaching judgment, although they may also symbolize the blood or persecution of the saints. The "harps of God" perhaps suggest that God won the victory and that in turn his people will use them to praise him.

The "song of Moses" (v. 3) probably refers to Exodus 15:1-18, although there is another song of Moses in Deuteronomy 32:1-43. Yet the words quoted in verses 3-4 do not closely resemble either song of Moses, but include a composite of several Old Testament passages. Whether John meant that the song of Moses and the "song of the Lamb" were two different songs or the same is not clear. Whatever the case, the song as presented by John praises God for his greatness, power, righteousness, truth, and deeds. Instead of "King of the ages," the most reliable Greek manuscripts read, "King of the nations," although a few late manuscripts have "King of the saints." Verse 4 may indicate a contrast between the greatness of God and that of the beast (13:4). The statement "All nations shall come and worship thee" seems to contradict the unrepentant attitude of unregenerate people depicted elsewhere (9:20-21; 20:7-9). However, the word translated "worship" means to prostrate oneself before another, either sincerely or insincerely. At any rate, this passage is wrongly interpreted when it is used to support the unbiblical doctrine of universal salvation.

Angels Prepare to Serve Plagues (15:5-8)

Next John saw that "the temple of the tent of witness in heaven was opened" (v. 5). The word for "temple" means sanctuary and here means the holy of holies in the tabernacle, which was a prototype of the three succeeding Jewish Temples. The tabernacle, and the holy of holies in particular, symbolized the presence of God. Both Jews and Christians (Heb. 8:1-5) believed in a heavenly counterpart of the earthly tabernacle or Temple. However, we shall note later that there is no temple in heaven (21:22).

The fact that the holy of holies "was opened" suggests the accessibility to God of all his children because Christ, the perfect high priest, had offered the perfect sacrifice, himself. This truth was indicated by the tearing of the Temple's veil when Jesus died (Matt. 27:51). Since "the seven angels with the seven plagues" came out of the temple (v. 6), they probably were identical with "the seven angels who stand before God" (8:2). They had on priestly garments, which likely symbolized purity, holiness, and perhaps royalty. "One of the four living creatures," symbolic of all living things, "gave the seven angels seven golden bowls full of the wrath of God who lives for ever and ever" (v. 7). Since to reject God's love is to receive his wrath, the eternal law of sin and retribution must eventually run its course. According to Old Testament usage, "smoke" symbolized God's presence and glory and also depicted a certain hiddenness of God even when he revealed himself (v. 8*a*). The reason that "no one could enter the temple until the seven plagues of the seven angels were ended" may be God's majestic and awesome presence or the fact that God's judgment is so fixed and certain that no one now can intercede on behalf of the wicked (v. 8*b*).

First Bowl: Against the Earth (16:1-2)

The task of interpreting the seven seals, seven trumpets, and seven bowls is similar to the task of interpreting Jesus' great eschatalogical discourse (Matt. 24:1-44). For example, Jesus answered his disciples' threefold question concerning the destruction of the Temple, the sign of his coming, and the sign of the end of the age in such a way that working out an exact chronological sequence is impossible. Likewise, John's succession of seals, trumpets, and bowls all three cover the same time span, from the first advent to the second advent of Christ. Perhaps our greatest problem in interpretation stems from attempting to match John's apocalyptic descriptions with particular historical events. Futurists have a still greater problem when they attempt to apply the content of the seals, trumpets, and bowls only to the time span related to Christ's second coming. On the other hand, preterists and others whose views are basically oriented to the past tend to avoid what should be obvious to all, that Revelation does depict the consummation of all history, not only just that of the ancient Roman empire.

The bowl judgments and the trumpet judgments are similar in some ways and different in others. The trumpet judgments included mercy, thus calls to repentance. In the bowl judgments, the wicked are beyond hope of repentance. The trumpet judgments were only partially destructive, whereas the bowl judgments are complete and final. In the trumpet judgments, mankind was affected only indirectly until the fifth trumpet. Yet all the bowl judgments directly affect mankind. Like the seals and trumpets, the bowls fall into the following grouping: four bowls, two bowls, an interlude, and one bowl.

The "loud voice from the temple" probably came from God, who directed the seven angels: "Go and pour out on the earth the seven bowls of the wrath of God." God's wrath no longer is tempered by mercy. His patience has reached an end. The bowls of wrath are reminiscent of Jeremiah 25:15, which also denotes God's judgment on the nations. The first bowl judgment is similar to the sixth plague against Egypt (Ex. 9:8-12). According to John's description, "foul and evil sores came upon the men who bore the mark of the beast and worshiped its image" (v. 2). Although some interpret the first bowl judgment to symbolize mental and spiritual problems, there should be no objection to taking it to mean physical sores. Whether specific sins produced the sores as a direct result of the nature of the sins cannot be determined. Since the earth, not just a part of it, was affected, this first judgment was universal. However, we cannot discover one or several particular historical incidents that correspond with the first or other six bowl judgments. Yet their cumulative effect caused the downfall of imperial Rome and eventually will effect the collapse of the entire world system.

Second Bowl: Against the Sea (16:3)

Like the first Egyptian plague (Ex. 7:14-25) and similar to the second trumpet's effect (8:8-9), the second bowl judgment involved turning water into blood. However, while the second trumpet affected only a third of the sea, the second bowl judgment included the entire sea, the result being that "it became like the blood of a dead man, and every living thing died that was in the sea." Since blood was the symbol of life, the "blood of a dead man" would indicate death and putrefaction accompanied by a foul odor. Since mankind is dependent upon nature for livelihood, when nature fails to provide the means of sustenance, mankind must die.

Third Bowl: Against the Fresh Waters (16:4-7)

Again like the first Egyptian plague, and also like the effect of the third trumpet, the fresh waters became blood as the result of the

third bowl judgment. As indicated in our interpretation of the
trumpet judgments against nature, God uses natural disasters to
accomplish his purpose. One aspect of God's purpose is his judgment of evil. According to verse 5, John "heard the angel of water
say, 'Just art thou in these thy judgments, thou who art and wast, O
Holy One.'"

Verse 6 states the main reason for judgment, particularly against
imperial Rome. Those who had "shed the blood of saints and
prophets" now must drink blood as their just due. Wicked people
now reap what they sowed according to God's inevitable moral law.
In reality, people do not break God's laws; rather, God's laws break
them. Just as those who defy the natural law of gravity will suffer a
painful fall, those who violate God's moral laws must suffer the
painful consequences. The unusual fact that John heard the "altar
cry" reminds us of Abel's blood crying out of the ground (Gen. 4:10).
Likewise, the martyrs under the heavenly altar (6:9-10) approved
the vindication of God's "true and just . . . judgments" (v. 7).

The Fourth Bowl: Against the Sun (16:8-9)

Unlike the fourth trumpet plague, which reduced the sun's light
by a third (8:12), the fourth bowl judgment intensified the heat of
the sun "to scorch men with fire" (v. 8). No Egyptian plague
parallels this event. Although the Egyptians and others worshiped
the sun, the Hebrews never considered it more than a symbol for
God. Malachi wrote that "the day comes, burning like an oven,
when all the arrogant and all evildoers will be stubble; the day that
comes shall burn them up, says the Lord of hosts" (4:1). In the very
next verse, Malachi added, "But for you who fear my name the sun
of righteousness shall rise, with healing in its wings" (4:2). Paradoxically, light both enlightens and blinds. Thus, Jesus said, "For
judgment I came into this world, that those who do not see may see,
and that those who see may become blind" (John 9:39). Instead of
their punishment moving them to repentance, wicked mankind
"cursed the name of God who had power over these plagues, and
they did not repent and give him glory" (v. 9b). Like Pharaoh, the

more they resisted God the more hardened their hearts became.

Fifth Bowl: Against the Throne of the Beast (16:10-11)

The "throne of the beast" probably refers to Rome, the capital of the Roman empire. We must remember, however, that Rome was only one of many past and future examples of the corrupt world system. If Rome fell, the entire Roman empire would fall. The result of the fifth bowl plague was that the beast's "kingdom was in darkness," which is reminiscent of the ninth Egyptian plague (Ex. 10:21-23). According to scriptural usage, darkness often symbolizes sin, ignorance, and moral corruption (John 3:19-20; Rom. 2:19). Some see in the fifth bowl judgment a parallel to the fifth trumpet plague, which included darkness caused by grotesque, locust-like creatures (9:1-11). The words "men gnawed their tongues in anguish" (v. 10*b*) normally would indicate intense physical pain, but some interpreters hold that the description symbolizes mental or spiritual pain. Perhaps it includes both. Again we note that punishment did not lead to repentance. Rather, the wicked blamed God, not themselves, for their trouble, as they continued to curse God.

Sixth Bowl: Against Euphrates as Prelude to Armageddon (16:12-16)

At the blowing of the sixth trumpet, we noted the loosing of the four angels bound at the Euphrates River and the subsequent invasion by a tremendous cavalry numbering 200,000,000 (9:13-21). Again we see the prominence of the Euphrates as "its water was dried up, to prepare the way for the kings from the east" (v. 12). The description reminds us of the drying up of the Red Sea (Ex. 14:21) and the Jordan (Josh. 3:17). Later Cyrus, the great Persian king, diverted the Euphrates, which ran through Babylon, in order to capture the city. As we noted earlier, the Euphrates was the northern boundary of Israel and the eastern boundary of Rome. If John had in mind the invasion of imperial Rome, the "kings from the east" very well may refer to the Parthians. Modern futurists may view them as either Russians, Chinese, or both.

John saw "issuing from the mouth of the dragon and from the mouth of the beast and from the mouth of the false prophet, three foul spirits like frogs" (v. 13). Although this is the first reference to the "false prophet," we shall see in 19:20 that he was the second or land beast (13:11). Whether the dragon, beast, and false prophet are to be viewed as an unholy trinity, thus a parody of the heavenly Trinity, is not certain, but seems quite likely. Although the second Egyptian plague was frogs (Ex. 8:1-15), the similarity between that event and the present "three foul spirits like frogs" may be limited to the concept of uncleanness. According to verse 14, "they are demonic spirits, performing signs, who go abroad to the kings of the whole world, to assemble them for battle on the great day of God the Almighty." Possibly the three froglike spirits are symbolic of false teachings or propaganda, which satanic forces historically have used in their attempt to impede and frustrate the purposes of God. Not only imperial Rome and its forces, but the entire world system of all time has opposed and will continue to oppose God until he overthrows it completely and finally.

Reference to "the great day of God the Almighty" is John's way of designating "the day of the Lord," mentioned numerous times by the Old Testament prophets (Isa. 13:9; Jer. 46:10; Joel 3:14). Most of the references depict God's judgment upon the godless nations. The Israelites generally thought that God would vindicate them on that day when God would break into history. However, Amos in particular warned that sinning Israelites also would be the objects of divine judgment (Amos 5:18-20). In one sense, the day of the Lord came at the incarnation (Acts 2:17-21, quoting Joel 2:28-32). Yet the fullest expression of the day of the Lord will be at Christ's second coming, when he returns as judge (Matt. 25:31-46; 2 Cor. 5:10). Thus, verse 15 injects the words of the glorified Christ: "Lo, I am coming like a thief! Blessed is he who is awake, keeping his garments that he may not go naked and be seen exposed!" This statement serves two purposes: encouragement for the saints and a warning for the wicked.

In his earthly ministry, Jesus taught that he would return unexpectedly and compared his coming to that of a thief in his parable of the householder (Matt. 24:42-51; 25:13). Later Paul wrote

that Jesus would return "like a thief in the night" (1 Thess. 5:2).
Reference to watchfulness reminds us of Christ's words to the
church at Sardis, in which he also said he would "come as a thief"
(3:2-3). Likewise, reference to "keeping his garments that he may
not go naked" reminds us of Christ's words to the Laodicean church
(3:18). The garments refer to spiritual clothing, which only Christ
can provide. Although there are many judgments against nations in
history, one day Christ climactically is coming to bring history to a
close and to judge all mankind in terms of vindicating the righteous
and punishing the wicked.

Although the battle of Armageddon awaits description in chapter
19:19-21, we have the announcement of it here in verse 16. The
meaning of Armageddon is uncertain. The most logical solution is
that the prefix *ar* is a smooth form (no "h" sound) of the Hebrew *har*,
meaning "mountain." Accordingly, Armageddon means mountain
or hill of Megiddo. Geographically, however, Megiddo is the name
of a plain, not a mountain. Yet the plain of Megiddo is near Mount
Carmel, and perhaps John applied the name Megiddo to the
mountain in order to tie it to Ezekiel's prediction of God's destruction of "Gog, of the land of Magog" (38:2) in the mountains of Israel
(Ezek. 38:1 to 39:29).

Rather than interpret Armageddon as a flesh and blood military
slugfest, the name has become symbolic of all decisive battles. John
probably chose the name because of the bloody history of the plain
of Megiddo in the valley of Esdraelon. Gideon and his men defeated
the Midianites in this general area (Judg. 6:33ff.). The Philistines
defeated Saul and his army at Mount Gilboa nearby (1 Sam. 31:1).
Barak and Deborah defeated Sisera's forces there (Judg. 5:19-21). At
Megiddo, Ahaziah died from Jehu's arrows (2 Kings 9:27). There
Pharaoh Neco killed Josiah (2 Kings 23:29), whose death became for
Israel a symbol of deep sorrow and mourning (Zech. 12:11).
Armageddon symbolizes both the defeat of Rome and ultimately the
defeat of the whole of evil world power.

Seventh Bowl: Against the Air,
Bringing Disasters (16:17-21)

Just as the seventh seal and the seventh trumpet represented not only the end of a series but implied an end of history, the seventh bowl more emphatically suggests the absolute end of things, as "a loud voice" (apparently God's) from the temple's throne said, "It is done!" (literally, "It has come to pass"). Just as prophetic utterances often have a dual meaning, this declaration has a dual meaning. On the lower level, it meant the end of imperial Rome. Yet, on the higher level, it meant the end of all human history. Since the "seventh angel poured his bowl into the air" (v. 17), all of nature (earth, sea, fresh waters, sun, and now the air) had turned against wicked mankind. According to scriptural usage, the air, as well as the world, was the domain of Satan (Eph. 2:2). Paul's statement that believers will meet the Lord in the air (1 Thess. 4:17) may imply Christ's triumph over Satan. The symbolism of "lightning," "thunder," and an "earthquake" (v. 18) indicates divine judgment. Whether John meant that natural disasters contributed to the fall of Rome, or he simply employed natural phenomena altogether symbolically, is uncertain. However, history discloses that natural disasters, internal corruption, and external forces were principal reasons for the downfall of imperial Rome.

In verse 19, we read that "The great city was split into three parts, and the cities of the nations fell." We assume that the "great city" means Rome, but mention of the "cities of the nations" must point to the ultimate defeat of the entire world system. We can only guess as to the symbolism of "three parts." Since three is the number for deity, it may indicate the divine source of Rome's destruction. We interpret "great Babylon" also to mean Rome in particular and the entire world system in general. Instead of "to make her drain the cup of the fury of his wrath," (v. 19) an exact translation is "to give her the cup of the wine of the anger of his wrath." The obvious meaning of either translation is complete and thorough judgment. The apocalyptic language of verses 20-21 stresses the awesome devastation of divine judgment. The seventh Egyptian plague was hail (Ex. 9:22-26), and hailstones attributed to God helped Joshua defeat the Amorites (Josh. 10:11). Thus, hail was another symbol of divine judgment. The fact that these hailstones each weighed a hundred pounds merely serves to emphasize the awesome devastation of God's judgment. Yet, as we have seen repeatedly, evil men cursed God instead of admitting the error of their ways by repenting of their sins.

Fall of Babylon—Rome
17:1 to 19:5

The Harlot and the Beast (17:1-6)

One of the seven angels that had the seven bowls invited John to see "the judgment of the great harlot who is seated upon many waters" (v. 1). In the immediate context, the "great harlot" refers to the city of Rome, though her name is Babylon according to verse 5. Ancient Babylon, which became a symbol not only for Rome but for every manifestation of ungodly world power, indeed sat "upon many waters." For example, the Euphrates River ran through Babylon, and Babylon was famous for its many irrigation canals. Although only the Tiber River ran through Rome, as the seat of the vast empire, Rome also sat upon many waters. The symbol of harlotry for a sinful city was common in the Old Testament: Nineveh (Nah. 3:4), Tyre (Isa. 23:17), Jerusalem (Isa. 1:21; Jer. 2:20). The vivid description of the kings of the earth committing fornication with the harlot depicts not only commerce and culture but also the cooperation of Rome's vassal rulers in carrying out the policies of Rome (v. 2). Since the "dwellers on earth" obviously are followers of the beast, their becoming drunk on the wine of her fornication (14:8) points to Rome's idolatry and may refer particularly to their participation in the persecution of Christians.

In a supernatural state of inspiration, John was "carried . . . away in the Spirit into a wilderness" where he "saw a woman sitting on a scarlet beast which was full of blasphemous names, and it had seven heads and ten horns" (v. 3). Mention of a wilderness may point to the fact that biblical men of God often had their deepest spiritual experiences in isolated or desolate places. If the woman was the city of Rome, the "scarlet beast" was the Roman Empire, scarlet possibly denoting persecution or merely the splendor of the empire. Reference to blasphemous names probably means the assumption of divine names by the Roman emperors. Like the dragon (12:3), the beast had "seven heads and ten horns." These symbols probably denote great wisdom (possibly a false claim to divine wisdom), and complete human power or power over all humanity. John, however, chose to vary the meaning of his symbols. For example, he explained that the seven heads referred to both "seven mountains" (v. 9) and "seven kings" (v. 10), whereas the ten horns referred to "ten kings" (v. 12). Verse 4 describes the "woman," no doubt to be contrasted with the radiant woman of chapter 12, as an overdressed, bejeweled seductress. Since biblical language equates idolatry with spiritual adultery, the "golden cup full of abominations and the impurities of her fornication" probably refers to Rome's gross idolatry. John derived his colorful description from the Old Testament depiction of ancient Babylon (Jer. 51:7). Like harlots who had their names inscribed on their headbands, this harlot advertised her "name of mystery: 'Babylon the great, mother of harlots and of earth's abominations'" (v. 5). In addition to Rome's idolatry, the city also had the reputation for gross immorality. Consequently, Rome was guilty of both spiritual and physical adultery. However, the fact that the woman was "drunk with the blood of the saints and the blood of the martyrs of Jesus" shows that John's main interest was with Rome's idolatry, particularly emperor worship with its accompanying persecution of Christians (v. 6a).

Why John "marveled greatly" is not altogether clear (v. 6b). Perhaps he was merely amazed by the terrible mixture of raw power and moral corruption, or possibly he wondered why the sovereign God would permit immoral, impudent Rome to run roughshod over his own people.

Mystery of the Harlot and the Beast (17:7-14)

The angel said that he would tell John the "mystery of the woman, and of the beast with seven heads and ten horns that carries her" (v. 7). First, the angel explained that the beast "was, and is not, and is to ascend from the bottomless pit and go to perdition" (v. 8a). The description suggests the Nero *redivivus* legend, as we shall note further. The followers of the beast, "whose names have not been written in the book of life . . . will marvel to behold the beast, because it was and is not and is to come" (v. 8b). The angel did not offer an easy solution to the mystery as he said, "This calls for a mind of wisdom: the seven heads are seven mountains on which the woman is seated; they are also seven kings, five of whom have fallen, one is, the other has not yet come, and when he comes he must remain only a little while. As for the beast that was and is not, it is an eighth but it belongs to the seven, and goes to perdition" (vv. 9-11). Like the number of the beast, this passage is one of the most challenging passages to interpreters. Those of the idealist or philosophy of history school are likely to say that the "seven mountains" symbolize powerful nations but not specific nations. Likewise, the "seven kings" are symbolic references to great earthly power as expressed throughout history, not to any particular period in history. Futurists and preterists alike identify the "seven mountains" as the seven hills on which Rome is located. They differ, however, as to time. Futurists insist on an end-time Rome, while preterists are equally certain that the passage refers to imperial Rome.

Many futurists believe that the "seven kings" really mean seven kingdoms or world empires. For example, one scheme is as follows: Five fallen—Egypt, Assyria, Babylon, Medo-Persia, Greece; one is—Rome; seventh—Christian Roman empire of Germanic nations; eighth—kingdom of the end-time Antichrist, which is a reconstitution of the Roman Empire, thus "belongs to the seven." Two obvious weaknesses are the identity of the seventh as the so-called Holy Roman Empire of the Middle Ages and the assumption that the Roman Empire will be reconstituted in the end time. Preterists also have a problem in identifying the "seven kings" with seven emperors. According to the most convincing arrangement, we find: Five fallen—Augustus, Tiberius, Caligula, Claudius, Nero; one is—Vespasian; seventh—Titus (who reigned only two years); eighth—Domitian, who "belongs to the seven" because as a persecutor he in effect was Nero reincarnated. This view also has two weaknesses: the omission of Galba, Otho, and Vitellius and the fact that John obviously did not write during the reign of Vespasian. Yet, in defense of the view, is the fact that Galba, Otho, and Vitellius had a combined reign of only about a year and thus were little more than pretenders. Moreover, since John's description otherwise was so obvious, some believe that he pretended to write during Vespasian's reign in order to deceive the Romans. The view that John had his vision during Vespasian's reign but wrote it down during Domitian's, seems contrived. Also, the view that John meant seven types of

Roman rule (kings, consuls, dictators, decemvirs, tribunes, emperors, an alleged Oriental type of government under Diocletian, and the eighth the kingdom of the end-time Antichrist) seems to have little merit. Despite the problems, it is best to understand that John referred to Roman emperors, the eighth being Domitian.

According to verse 12, the "ten horns . . . are ten kings who have not yet received royal power, but they are to receive authority as kings for one hour, together with the beast." Naturally, one's general approach determines the interpretation of these ten kings. Some present-day futurists have identified these kings with the nations of the European common market, but such a view is more sensational than logical. This writer believes that John had in mind certain puppet rulers of imperial Rome, the "one hour" referring to an indefinite but brief period of time. Verse 13 indicates that the ten kings unanimously supported the Roman government, particularly in Rome's effort to "make war on the Lamb" (v. 14a). However, despite the solidarity of his enemies, "the Lamb will conquer them, for he is Lord of lords and King of kings, and those with him are called and chosen and faithful" (v. 14b). As Jesus said to Pilate, "You would have no power over me unless it had been given you from above" (John 19:11), Domitian and his vassals existed only because of God's permissive will. The Lamb as "Lord of lords and King of kings" has the full authority of God (Deut. 10:17). Jesus' followers will share in his victory over evil forces. They are "called" (including both the invitation and the acceptance), "chosen" (elected by God but allowing for human freedom of choice), and "faithful" (committed to God and trustworthy).

War Against the Harlot (17:15-18)

Just as the sea symbolized multitudes of people (13:1), the angel explained to John: "The waters that you saw . . . are peoples and multitudes and nations and tongues" (v. 15). After supporting Rome for a time, "The ten horns . . . and the beast will hate the harlot" and "will make her desolate and naked, and devour her flesh and burn her up with fire" (v. 16). Although the Roman emperors seemed to be for Rome, their sinful excesses, accompanied by external enemies, led to her downfall. As lustful men use and then discard a harlot, the combined enemies of Rome will completely ravage Rome and thereby carry out God's purpose (v. 17). Even as God in the Old Testament era used nations to accomplish his will, he will use both Rome's rulers and pagan invaders to judge Rome. Yet in doing so God will work out his purpose through the free choices of the persons involved.

Announcement of Rome's Fall (18:1-3)

John recorded that he "saw another angel coming down from heaven, having great authority; and the earth was made bright with his splendor" (v. 1). The description suggests that the angel was from God and carried the authority of God. The idea of brightness implies the angel's recent association with God, just as Moses' face shone after coming down from Mount Sinai (Ex. 34:29). The content of the angel's pronouncement of doom upon Rome includes a medley of quotations from Old Testament taunt songs or doom songs against ancient Babylon in particular and also against other wicked cities. The words, "Fallen, fallen is Babylon the great!" (v. 2*a*), are identical to Isaiah 21:9 except for "the great." The additional description (vv. 2*b*-3) is similar to Isaiah 13:20-22. According to Jewish thought, demons inhabited deserted buildings and dry areas (Matt. 12:43). Reference to "every foul and hateful bird" seems to be drawn from Jeremiah 50:39: "Therefore wild beasts shall dwell with hyenas in Babylon, and ostriches shall dwell in her."

Verse 3 states three reasons for Rome's judgment: (1) "for all nations have drunk the wine of her impure passion"; (2) "the kings of the earth have committed fornication with her"; (3) "the merchants of the earth have grown rich with the wealth of her wantonness." The first charge seems to refer particularly to the sins of arrogance, pride, and the intoxicating power of wealth. The second charge probably relates more directly to the idolatrous worship promoted by Rome, and the third charge specifically stresses sinful excesses related to wealth.

Some futurists believe that Babylon will be rebuilt and destroyed in the future. Others believe that Rome, symbolized by the name of Babylon, will again achieve empire status in the future before being destroyed. Certain historicists, with whom this writer disagrees, identify Babylon (Rome) with the Roman Catholic Church. On the other hand, those who hold the idealist or philosophy of history view interpret Babylon to designate sinful human society, including its false religions, at any point in history, which eventually will fall as the result of the moral law of sowing and reaping. Throughout this commentary, the paradoxical view that the immediate application is to the imperial Rome that John knew, but the godless society represented by Rome will continue to reincarnate itself until it is finally and permanently overthrown by God is seen as correct. According to this view, Revelation was relevant to John's first readers, has been relevant in subsequent history, and will continue to be relevant until God rings down the final curtain of history and ushers in his eternal kingdom.

Christians to Leave Rome (18:4-8)

According to verse 4, John "heard another voice from heaven saying, 'Come out of her, my people, lest you take part in her sins, lest you share in her plagues.'" God's intention always has been that his people should be a separate people. The biblical emphasis on separation is spiritual in nature, not physical. The last part of verse 4 is a warning to all who participate in the sin of the world, since those who share in sin must also share in sin's judgment. Accordingly, Paul wrote, "you are slaves of the one whom you obey, either of sin, which leads to death, or of obedience, which leads to righteousness" (Rom. 6:16).

Verse 5 stresses the extent of Rome's sins as "heaped high as heaven," which is possibly an allusion to the account of the tower of Babel (Gen. 11:4). At least, both the people who built Babel and the leaders of Rome shared in common both pride and arrogance, coupled with rebellion against God. The fact that "God has remembered her iniquities" shows that God does not overlook sin and eventually will punish unrepentant sinners. The words "Render to her as she herself has rendered" (v. 6a) underline the truth that people reap what they sow (Gal. 6:7) and will be judged as they themselves have judged (Matt. 7:2). The idea of doubling Rome's punishment (v. 6b) stresses the completeness of Rome's punishment, perhaps implying that sin is accumulative in its effects. Thus, people not only reap later than they sow, but they also reap more than they sow, because sin, like grain, bears more fruit than the amount planted. This truth, however, does not suggest that God's punishment is capricious, arbitrary, and excessive. Only a casual reading of Isaiah 47:7-9 shows the close similarity between the Old Testament doom song against Babylon and John's indictment of Rome. Just as haughty Babylon was destroyed because of her sins, Rome will meet a similar fate, as "she shall be burned with fire; for mighty is the Lord God who judges her" (v. 8*b*).

Kings Lament Rome's Fall (18:9-10)

The "kings of the earth, who committed fornication and were wanton with her" (v. 9*a*), were not the ones who turned against Rome. Rather, they were those who cooperated with Rome in terms of trade, emperor worship, and other matters that were mutually beneficial. The fact that they "weep and wail over her" during her destruction may represent genuine concern for Rome. Yet their main concern probably was for themselves. The words "they will stand far off, in fear of her torment" (v. 9*b*) suggest disassociation because of fear that they too will share in Rome's destruction. Their lament expresses amazement that mighty Rome will be toppled "In one hour," a brief period of time. As pride goes before a fall, so it was with imperial Rome.

Merchants Lament Rome's Fall (18:11-17*a)*

The motive of the lament of "the merchants of the earth" apparently was selfishness. Instead of genuine concern for Rome, they seemingly were concerned only for their economic loss. The twenty-eight items of trade serve to emphasize the tremendous extent of Rome's commerce. Efforts to group them vary and are somewhat arbitrary. Unfortunately, "slaves, that is, human souls [lives]," were among the items of trade (v. 13). As a harlot plies her trade to obtain splendid clothing, jewelry, and expensive perfume and then loses everything when cast aside, thus Rome will forever lose all her "dainties and . . . splendor" (v. 14). Like the kings, the merchants "stand far off" as they lament Rome's destruction (v. 15). Yet the merchants' main interest was in their own economic loss as expressed in their lament, "In one hour all this wealth has been laid waste" (v. 17*a*).

Seamen Lament Rome's Fall (18:17*b*-20)

"And all shipmasters and seafaring men, sailors and all whose trade is on the sea, stood far off" (v. 17*b*) and lamented Rome's destruction with the rhetorical question, "What city was like the great city?" (v. 18). Throwing "dust on their heads" was a symbolic act of severe distress (v. 19*a*). Like the merchants, the seamen seemed mainly interested in their own economic loss, as they cried, "Alas, alas, for the great city where all who had ships at sea grew rich by her wealth!" (v. 19*b*). Although the Revised Standard Version includes verse 20 as coming from the lips of the seamen, the content seems to demand that the words were spoken by the angel or by John himself. The invitation was for "heaven . . . saints and apostles and prophets" to rejoice because God had judged Rome on their behalf. Perhaps the joy was more for the vindication of divine righteousness than for the realization of Rome's destruction. Yet we cannot rule out the latter.

Rome to Fall Like a Millstone (18:21-23)

In an impressive symbolic act, "a mighty angel took up a stone like a great millstone and threw it into the sea, saying, 'So shall Babylon the great city be thrown down with violence, and shall be found no more'" (v. 21). Some insist that the destruction of imperial Rome was not as complete as this imagery suggests. Since the city of Rome still exists today, these interpreters argue for a fulfillment yet future. However, we need to recognize that in the Scriptures overstatement or hyperbole is sometimes used (Matt. 19:24; John

21:25). Also, we suggest that Rome's destruction was symbolic of the eventual destruction of the forces of evil.

Entertainment Destroyed (18:22a)

John particularly seemed to have municipal Rome in mind as he recorded, "and the sound of harpers and minstrels, of flute players and trumpeters, shall be heard in thee no more." Rome's famed entertainment life was now conspicuous for its absence. No music indicated no life.

Industry Destroyed (18:22b)

The awesome description needs no interpretation: "and a craftsman of any craft shall be found in thee no more; and the sound of the millstone shall be heard in thee no more." The wheels of industry had come to a complete halt.

Home Life Destroyed (18:23a)

Since cities are conspicuous at night by their many lights (Matt. 5:14), the description "and the light of a lamp shall shine in thee no more" shows the desolation of Rome. A yet sadder statement discloses that "the voice of bridegroom and bride shall be heard in thee no more." Without family life, there can be no life, only death.

Commerce Destroyed (18:23b)

Although Rome's "merchants were the great men of the earth," they necessarily perished with Rome, which had deceived all nations with her sorcery.

Reason for Rome's Fall (18:24)

As varied and vicious as were Rome's sins, her greatest sin stemmed from enforced emperor worship, as expressed in the words, "And in her was found the blood of prophets and of saints, and of all who have been slain on the earth." Possibly the reference to Rome's deception of the nations (v. 23b) should be taken as part of the reason for her destruction. This view is particularly appropriate if we interpret the deception to refer to emperor worship. Someone has suggested that the blood of the martyrs was the seed of the church, meaning that persecution led to growth. While this assumption is at least partially true, we can say emphatically with John that the blood of the martyrs was the seed of Rome's destruction.

Heavenly Rejoicing over Rome's Fall (19:1-5)

Although historically Rome had not yet fallen, theologically she had. Rome's destruction was as certain as the promise of God and the inevitability of the outworking of God's moral law of sowing and reaping. John "heard what seemed to be the loud voice of a great multitude in heaven" (v. 19a). The "great multitude" may refer to the vast angelic host (5:11), to the great multitude of the redeemed (7:9), or perhaps to both. Their message was a great chorus of praise to God. The word "Hallelujah" is the Hebrew form of "Praise Jah [short for Yahweh]" or "Praise the Lord." All four occurrences of "Hallelujah" in the New Testament are here in chapter 19 (vv. 1, 3-4,6). The first of these praises God for his "Salvation and glory and power" (v. 1b) and "for his judgments," particularly his judgment of "the great harlot," Rome (v. 2). "Salvation," as used here, means complete deliverance from sin, that is, from sin's penalty, power, and presence. God's "glory" in its most developed sense refers to his character but here probably includes the majesty and brilliance associated with his person. God's "power" denotes his ability to accomplish his purpose, including both salvation and judgment or "judgments," which "are true and just."

Only God is a perfect judge for four reasons: (1) He alone knows all the facts; (2) he alone knows the motives behind the facts; (3) he alone is free from sin and thus able to judge impartially; and (4) he alone has the wisdom to judge righteously and the power to enforce his judgments perfectly. Rome's judgment was deserved for two reasons: (1) She "corrupted the earth with her fornication," and (2) she shed the blood of God's servants. As noted heretofore, Rome's "fornication" primarily was idolatry (false religion), particularly emperor worship.

The second "hallelujah" included praise for the fact that "The smoke from her goes up for ever and ever" (v. 3). Of course, this description is not literal but symbolic of Rome's complete and irreparable destruction. The language is almost identical to Isaiah's description of Edom's destruction (34:10). According to verse 4, "the twenty-four elders" (representing the totality of the redeemed) and "the four living creatures" (representing all of creation) "fell down and worshipped God . . . saying, 'Amen, Hallelujah!'" The word "Amen" means truly, surely, certainly. In this last appearance of the twenty-four elders and the four living creatures, we find them giving hearty agreement to the vindication of God's righteousness by his judgment upon Rome. Next we note that "from the throne came a voice crying, 'Praise our God, all you his servants, you who fear him, small and great'" (v. 5). Perhaps the unidentified voice was that of Christ himself, one of the elders, or one of the living creatures (cherubim). Whether "his servants" refers to martyrs (v. 2) and prophets (10:7) in particular, or to all of God's servants in general, is uncertain, although the latter seems more likely. Certainly the words, "small and great" include all believers, regardless of their social status or the extent of their service.

The Lamb's Final Triumph
19:6 to 20:15

The Marriage Feast (19:6-10)

Again John "heard what seemed to be the voice of a great multitude" (v. 6a), possibly the same one mentioned in 19:1, although the description of the voice is much more dramatic here. The fourth "Hallelujah" appears, the reason given, "For the Lord our God the Almighty reigns" (v. 6b). The word "Almighty" means all-powerful or omnipotent and seems to be John's favorite word for God, since he used it nine times in Revelation. Perhaps John intended a contrast between the all-powerful God and the limited power of the Roman emperor. Although God in his sovereignty has always reigned, yet he has limited his power to permit human beings to have a freedom of choice. According to the Model Prayer, God's will is being fully done in heaven, with the hope that it also will be done on earth (Matt. 6:10). However, when John wrote that "God the Almighty reigns," he referred to the consummation of history after God has defeated all hostile powers. Writing from the divine viewpoint, John saw the eternal kingdom of God as if it had already been accomplished.

According to verse 7, "the marriage of the Lamb" also was an accomplished fact from the divine perspective. Just as the Old Testament prophets used the symbol of marriage to describe God's relationship to Israel (Isa. 54:5-6; Hos. 2:19-20), the New Testament emphasizes the marriage motif (Matt. 22:1-14; John 3:29; Eph. 5:23-32). Moreover, since joy was perhaps the chief characteristic of a wedding, so it is with the marriage of the Lamb, as indicated by the words "rejoice" and "exult." The expression, "his Bride has made herself ready," refers to the church in its broadest sense (the totality of the redeemed). The Bride has made herself ready by faith in Christ, by keeping herself morally unspotted from the world, and by fidelity to her divine Groom. In contrast with the lurid attire of the harlot (Rome, the earthly city), the Bride (the Holy City, the New Jerusalem) is "clothed with fine linen bright and pure," which "is the righteous deeds of the saints" (v. 8). The moral purity of the Bride contrasts sharply with the immorality of the harlot. The reference to "righteous deeds" does not mean that the saints merited their salvation. Rather, it shows that their works demonstrated or proved their faith.

Next, John's angelic narrator instructed him to write: "Blessed are those who are invited to the marriage supper of the Lamb," with the added words of assurance, "These are true words of God" (v. 9). In reality, the Bride (the redeemed) and the guests are the same. The Jewish apocryphal literature has much to say about a messianic banquet at the end of the age. Jesus alluded to such a banquet when he said, "I tell you, many will come from east and west and sit at table with Abraham, Isaac, and Jacob in the kingdom of heaven" (Matt. 8:11). Additionally, his statement at the Last Supper about drinking again of the fruit of the vine in his Father's kingdom pointed to the same concept. John's fourth "Blessed" (Beatitude) basically means happy or to be congratulated are those invited to the marriage supper of the Lamb. Whether the supper is literal or symbolic, it denotes a joyful occasion of intimate fellowship.

Apparently excited about the prospect of such fellowship, plus the assurance that the angel's message constituted "true words of God," John instinctively but thoughtlessly fell down at the angel's feet to worship him (v. 10a). The angel, however, quickly corrected the mistake by saying, "You must not do that! I am a fellow servant with you and your brethren who hold the testimony of Jesus. Worship God" (v. 10b). This incident perhaps served as a corrective against angel worship, which was characteristic of Gnosticism and possibly an extreme element in Judaism. Paul forbade the worship of angels (Col. 2:18). Since both angels and people are created beings whose purpose is to serve God, only God deserves worship. The statement "For the testimony of Jesus is the spirit of prophecy" (v. 10c) seems unrelated to the context. "Testimony of Jesus" may mean testimony he bore, testimony that others bore about him, or both. Twice John has described Jesus as the "faithful witness" (1:5; 3:14). Jesus was the supreme spokesman (prophet) of God (Heb. 1:1-2). In turn, his disciples are to proclaim faithfully the truth he taught and is.

The Lordship of Christ (19:11-16)

Although the marriage supper of the Lamb was announced, John's account implies a postponement until Christ has won the victory over his enemies. Apparently chapters 21—22 record its fulfillment. Yet the marriage symbol gives way to the descent from heaven of the new Jerusalem. John's statement that he "saw heaven opened" (v. 11a) may mean that he had a divinely given insight into God's plan. In this new vision, John saw a "white horse," and "He who sat upon it is called Faithful and True" (v. 11b). Unlike the rider of the white horse in 6:2, this rider clearly refers to Christ, as indicated by the description "Faithful" (1:5; 3:14) and "True" (3:7, 14). Christ is faithful in the sense that he keeps his promises and stands by his followers. In contrast with error and falsehood, Christ is always true. In contrast with what is a mere shadow or altogether transient and temporal, Christ is eternal, the ultimate reality, who solemnly affirmed, "I am the way, and the truth, and the life" (John 14:6). While John did not identify this scene with Christ's second coming, the fact that it leads to the consummation of the age implies as much. That he will return as both judge and warrior is indicated by the words, "in righteousness he judges and makes war" (v. 11c). As we saw earlier (1:14; 2:18), "His eyes are like a flame of fire" (v. 12a). This description suggests that his eyes penetrate into people's very thoughts, and thus he knows all about them. Whereas the dragon wore a diadem on each of seven heads (12:3) and the sea beast a diadem on each of ten horns (13:1), Christ has "on his head . . . many diadems" (v. 12b). Since a diadem is symbolic of kingly reign, Christ has all kingly authority, as indicated by "many" and later the affirmation in verse 16.

The meaning of his secret name, "which no one knows but himself," is much debated (v. 12c). Some believe it is the name Jesus or perhaps Yahweh, the covenant name, which the Jews held to be so sacred they refused to say it and even forgot how to pronounce it. Another idea is that Christ's name (whether Jesus, the title Lord, or some other) is so rich in meaning that our finite minds simply cannot grasp its fullness (Matt. 11:27). According to Jewish thought, one's name stood for one's person. Thus, to believe in Jesus' name is to believe in him. Also, in Jewish thought, knowing the name of a person in some sense gave the knower certain influence with or over the one known (Gen. 32:29; Judg. 13:18). For example, Jesus asked the Gerasene demoniac, "What is your name?" (Luke 8:30). Although knowing Jesus' name may give one influence with him because of the faith relationship involved, yet no one has authority over him.

Verse 13 describes Christ as having his "robe dipped in blood." While some believe the blood was his own or perhaps that of the martyrs, the context seems to demand that it refers to the blood of his enemies, either those already slain or about to be slain. Even though some view this scene as very un-Christlike, it must be remembered that the vision is symbolic, not literal. The picture is one of complete victory over his enemies. Verse 13 continues by relating that "the name by which he is called is The Word of God." John, in his Gospel, particularly identified Jesus as the Word, who both "was with God" and "was God" (1:1). The Old Testament concept of God's word is that it is dynamic and creative (Gen. 1:3) and accomplishes God's purpose (Isa. 55:10-11). Unlike warriors dressed for battle, John saw "the armies of heaven, arrayed in fine linen, white and pure," also riding "on white horses" (v. 14). As previously noted, white was symbolic of moral purity, perhaps also of victory. Presumably the armies symbolized the redeemed, though angelic forces also might have been included, as in the earlier vision.

According to verse 15, "From his mouth issues a sharp sword with which to smite the nations, and he will rule them with a rod of iron" (Ps. 2:9). As we noted earlier (1:16), the sword symbolizes the word of God, not a literal sword with which he will slash human bodies. Contrary to the view that "smite the nations" refers to their conversion, the military symbolism clearly seems to denote defeat, not conversion. Yet to go from symbolism to reality has its problems. Certainly Christ will not have to engage in a military slugfest to defeat his enemies. If he could create the world with his word, Christ should have no problem defeating his enemies with a word. When those who came to arrest Jesus in Gethsemane "drew back and fell to the ground" after Jesus identified himself, they realized something of his awesome presence and power (John 18:6). Reference to his treading "the wine press of the fury of the wrath of God the Almighty" (Isa. 63:3) depicts judgment and complete victory. "On his robe and on his thigh he has a name inscribed, King of kings and Lord of lords" (v. 16). Earlier we noted the same title in reverse order (17:14).

Overthrow of the Beast and False Prophet (19:17-21)

Although the gruesome scene depicted here is not called the battle of Armageddon, the clash between "the beast and the kings of the earth with their armies" and "him who sits upon the horse and . . . his army" (v. 19) clearly must be a fulfillment of the battle of Armageddon, earlier announced but not fought (16:16). The "angel standing in the sun" probably was universally seen and heard as he invited the birds to "Come, gather for the great supper of God, to eat the flesh of kings, the flesh of captains, the flesh of mighty men, the flesh of horses and their riders, and the flesh of all men, both free and slave, both small and great" (v. 18). We see here a contrast between this grisly supper and the marriage supper of the Lamb (v. 9). The language seemingly was borrowed from Ezekiel 39:17-20, which depicts the destruction of the armies of Gog and Magog.

Some interpret this great carnage literally while others take it symbolically of complete destruction. If we interpret this passage to refer both to the destruction of imperial Rome and also the final destruction of sinful society, perhaps the language is both literal and figurative. No doubt many dead bodies were consumed by the birds after the Germanic hordes had devastated Rome. Furthermore, when God does break into history again in the person of Christ to consummate salvation and to judge the wicked, somehow wicked people will die.

The so-called battle turns out to be no battle at all. The beast, the false prophet, and their forces were no match for Christ and his forces even though the latter's only weapon was God's Word. The beast and the false prophet "were thrown alive into the lake of fire that burns with sulphur" (v. 20). Although the Jewish apocalyptic literature has much to say on the subject, the Scriptures (particularly the New Testament) also have a great deal to say about the concept of hell in terms of fire. For example, Jesus spoke of "hell [gehenna], where their worm does not die, and the fire is not quenched" (Mark 9:47-48). In Jesus' story of the rich man and Lazarus, the rich man went to hades from which he said, "for I am in anguish in this flame" (Luke 16:24). Although the Hebrew Sheol (translated hades in Greek) refers to the shadowy abode of the dead and often means merely the grave, only in Luke's account of the rich man and Lazarus does hades ever designate a place of fiery punishment. In contrast, Jesus chose Gehenna (Greek for valley of Hinnom) to describe the final state of the wicked in terms of fire and punishment. Because of its association with gross idolatry, Josiah designated the valley of Hinnom as the official garbage dump of Jerusalem (2 Kings 23:10). Because of continual fire and decay, the valley of Hinnom became a fitting symbol to describe the final state of the wicked. In the Scriptures, fire is a frequent symbol of judgment.

The Binding of Satan (20:1-3)

John saw an unidentified "angel coming down from heaven, holding in his hand the key of the bottomless pit and a great chain" (v. 1). Earlier we noted a "star fallen from heaven to earth," to whom "was given the key of the shaft of the bottomless pit" (9:1). Later this so-called "star" apparently was identified as "the angel of the bottomless pit," whose name meant Destroyer and seemed to designate Satan (9:11). Thus, we assume the angel in the present passage is not the same as the one in chapter 9. The fact that it came "down from heaven" suggests that it had the authority of God. In both passages, the "key" symbolizes authority, and the "chain" symbolizes captivity, imprisonment, and curtailment of activity. Next the angel "seized the dragon, that ancient serpent, who is the Devil and Satan, and bound him for a thousand years, and threw him into the pit, and shut it and sealed it over him, that he should deceive the nations no more, till the thousand years were ended" (vv. 2-3a).

Because this passage raises so many controversial questions, interpretations vary greatly. Although futurists tend toward a more literal interpretation, some of them do not believe that Satan, a spiritual being, will be bound with a literal chain. Neither do all futurists believe in a literal thousand years, though they do believe it refers to a period of time. Others interpret a thousand in terms of numerology, that is, the cube of the number ten, the result being completeness and, consequently, not referring to time at all. However, the words "After that he must be loosed for a little while" (v. 3b) certainly suggest chronology. While the idea that the binding and loosing are different aspects of the same thing, and thus simultaneous, is intriguing, there is grave difficulty in relating it to the context. At least from Augustine (AD 354-430) onward, many interpreters have related this passage to Jesus' parable about a stronger person binding the strong man before plundering his house (Mark 3:27). Satan, of course, was the strong man, and Jesus was the one stronger than Satan. Some limit the binding of Satan to only the matter of deceiving the nations with reference to emperor worship, while others insist that Satan's activity was completely stopped during the thousand years.

The Millennium (20:4-10)

A thousand-year reign of Christ is mentioned only in the twentieth chapter of Revelation. Yet many build a complicated scheme of theology on the subject of the millennium (from the Latin *mille*, 1,000, and *annum*, year). The three main views of the millennium are known as postmillennial, premillennial, and amillennial. As the term implies, postmillennialists believe that Jesus will return after the millennium, which they interpret as a thousand years of peace resulting from the triumphant spread of the gospel.

The premillennial view holds that Christ will return before the millennium and set up an earthly reign from Jerusalem. With variation, the general order of events is: (1) rapture of the church and the resurrection of dead believers at the secret coming of Christ; (2) judgment seat of Christ for believers only, in the air; (3) Israel united in Palestine, perhaps earlier; (4) the great tribulation on earth, either for seven or three and one-half years; (5) the open coming of Christ; (6) the battle of Armageddon; (7) the millennium, while Satan is bound; (8) loosing and complete defeat of Satan and his forces; (9) resurrection of dead believers; (10) great white throne judgment, for unbelievers only; and (11) eternal bliss or punishment. Some premillennialists insert the judgment of the nations (Matt. 25:31-46) as a separate judgment prior to the start of the millennium. The dispensational type of premillennialism is more detailed.

The amillennial view holds that there is no actual or literal millennium. Rather, the millennium is symbolic or figurative, depicting an indefinite period of time, usually considered to be the period between the first and second advents of Christ. Others believe that the millennium does not refer to time at all. As for the reign of Christ, it is a spiritual, heavenly rule, not a political reign on earth. Most amillennialists believe in a general resurrection and a general judgment (both including believers and unbelievers).

Who are those John saw on "thrones . . . to whom judgment was committed" (v. 4a)? Daniel mentioned "thrones" but did not say who would sit on them when "the court sat in judgment" (7:9-10). Jesus promised his disciples: "when the Son of man shall sit on his glorious throne, you who have followed me will also sit on twelve thrones, judging the twelve tribes of Israel" (Matt. 19:28). Since John went on to write that he "saw the souls of those who had been beheaded for their testimony to Jesus and for the word of God" (v. 4b), many believe that only martyrs will sit on thrones and reign with Christ for a thousand years. However, others insist that John meant two groups when he added, "and who had not worshiped the beast or its image and had not received its mark on their foreheads or their hands" (v. 4c). Since all Christians were not put to death because they resisted emperor worship, surely the survivors were just as faithful as those who died and thus are to be included in the millennial reign. In a still broader context, it seems best to see that all believers of all time will be included.

Those who interpret "They came to life" (v. 4d) to mean only the martyrs consistently affirm that only martyrs will participate in the "first resurrection" (v. 5b). Yet no other Scripture hints of a special resurrection for martyrs only. Futurists hold that the "first resurrection" is a resurrection for all believers one thousand years before the implied, but not expressed, second resurrection. However, Jesus said, "for the hour is coming when all who are in the tombs will hear his voice and come forth, those who have done good, to the resurrection of life, and those who have done evil, to the resurrection of judgment" (John 5:28-29). Jesus seems to have meant a general resurrection, including believers and unbelievers of all time. In comparison, Paul always mentioned only the resurrection of believers. Frequently, however, the new birth or conversion experience is described as a resurrection. In Romans 6:3-4, Paul wrote that water baptism depicts a spiritual death and resurrection. In Ephesians 2:6, he wrote that God "raised us up with him," and in Colossians 2:12 that "you were buried with him in baptism, in which you were also raised with him through faith." This writer concludes, therefore, that the first resurrection is the resurrection of the new-birth experience, which water baptism symbolizes.

Who are "The rest of the dead" who "did not come to life until the thousand years were ended" (v. 5a)? Some say they refer to all the physically dead except the martyrs. Futurists limit them to the unregenerate physically dead. I agree with the futuristic view but with a different emphasis and without denying a general resurrection. As Ray Frank Robbins fittingly wrote, "The redeemed rise twice, and die but once, while the unredeemed rise but once and die twice."[1] To this writer this view has fewer difficulties than the others and better fits the overall biblical context. Thus, in his fifth Beatitude, John could say, "Blessed and holy is he who shares in the first resurrection! Over such the second death has no power" (v. 6a). Later, the "second death" is identified with eternal punishment in the "lake of fire" (v. 14). Those who have experienced the new birth "shall be priests of God and of Christ, and they shall reign with him a thousand years" (v. 6b). This spiritual reign with Christ will include the believer's earthly sojourn with Christ and will continue in heaven after physical death. Consequently, the thousand years seems best interpreted as symbolic of that period of time between the first and second advents of Christ.

Why "Satan will be loosed" after his thousand-year imprisonment is not clear (v. 7). Some believe the purpose is for testing those converted during the millennium to determine if their faith is genuine. Others see it as God's way of demonstrating the perverseness of the unregenerate heart. This latter view presupposes a literal, earthly millennium and also that many unregenerated people living under Christ's benevolent rule still will continue to rebel against him in their hearts and later will rally behind Satan when he "will come out to deceive the nations" (v. 8a).

According to George R. Beasley-Murray, "It is more than possible that John's reflections on Genesis 1—3 led him to the thought that as Satan was allowed to enter the first paradise to expose the nature of man's heart, in the restoration of paradise he will be permitted to do so again."[2] Genesis 10:2 informs us that Noah's son Japheth had a son named Magog. However, in Ezekiel 38:2, Gog is from the "land of Magog, the chief prince of Meshech and Tubal" (v. 8b). Chapters 38—39 of Ezekiel depict Gog and his forces as enemies of God. Just as Jezebel became symbolic of evil womanhood, Gog and Magog became symbolic of God's enemies. To identify them specifically is impossible, and those modern interpreters who attempt to link them with Russia are resorting to sensationalism. We note that Gog and Magog assembled their innumerable forces "for battle" (v. 8c). Then "they marched up over the broad earth and surrounded the camp of the saints and the beloved city; but fire came down from heaven and consumed them" (v. 9). Although many believe "the beloved city" refers to the earthly Jerusalem, it seems rather to refer to the heavenly Jerusalem. Earlier John had described earthly Jerusalem symbolically as Sodom and Egypt (11:8).

What appeared to be a great battle shaping up turned out to be no battle at all, as "fire came down from heaven and consumed them" (v. 9b). "Fire" is a common symbol for judgment. If the destruction was physical, as the text seems to indicate, the fire perhaps was real. Some, however, take this passage to mean spiritual judgment, fire thus being used figuratively. The fact that it "came down from heaven" shows that God was the source. Although the expression "consumed them" may suggest annihilation to some, the Scriptures do not teach the annihilation of the wicked. This passage, however, does teach the final defeat of the devil and his followers. No longer will he be able to deceive people. His fate included being "thrown into the lake of fire and sulphur where the beast and the false prophet were," and where the unholy three "will be tormented day and night for ever and ever" (v. 10). Regardless of whether this vivid description is to be interpreted literally or figuratively, we can be sure that God's actions are in full accord with perfect justice.

The Great White Throne Judgment (20:11-15)

John next saw "a great white throne," symbolizing purity, holiness, and justice (v. 11a). No doubt the one "who sat upon it" was God or Christ (v. 11b). Although we usually think of God the Father as judge, Jesus said that the Father had given all judgment to him (John 5:22). Yet, because of the unity of Father and Son, there is no contradiction if we interpret either or both Father and Son as the judge. The description that "earth and sky fled away" suggests the majesty and awesomeness of the judge; and the words "no place was found for them" represent apocalyptic language, pointing to the new heaven and new earth (v. 11c).

Next John "saw the dead, great and small, standing before the throne, and books were opened" (v. 12a). The picture here implies a general judgment rather than a judgment only for unbelievers. Apparently the "books" refer to the record of everyone's thoughts, words, and deeds. Whether the books are literal, or merely symbolize that God's omniscience includes all knowledge, is not important. The presence of the "book of life" implies that believers are present and also subject to judgment. However, since their sins already have been judged in the person of Jesus Christ, in the real sense of judgment, they will not be judged (John 5:24). "And the dead were judged by what was written in the books, by what they had done" (v. 12b). Contrary to the view of multiple judgments, this writer believes the judgment of the nations (Matt. 25:31-46), the "judgment seat of Christ" (2 Cor. 5:10), the "judgment seat of God" (Rom. 14:10-12), and the great white throne judgment all refer to the same judgment, which will include every person who has ever lived. Although people will be judged according to their works, their true character determines their works (Matt. 7:16-20). Final judgment apparently serves two purposes: (1) It vindicates God's righteousness, and (2) it confirms the eternal destiny of every person.

According to verse 13, "the sea gave up the dead in it, and Death and Hades gave up the dead in them, and all were judged by what they had done." Mention of the sea may reflect the importance the Hebrews and other ancient people put on proper burial. Consequently, even those submerged in the sea without proper burial will be present at this final judgment. "Death" refers to the realm of death, and "Hades" means the unseen world or spirit world. Thus, all the dead will assemble for the great white throne judgment. John seemingly personified both death and hades, which "were thrown into the lake of fire" (v. 14a). Since death is both man's common experience and his worst enemy, while hades, the realm of death, is man's common destiny, both death and Hades will be consigned to destruction. Their power over mankind is both limited and temporary. John identified the "lake of fire" as the "second death," that is, eternal separation from God (v. 14b). The first death, of course, is physical death. Eternal separation from God will be the final destiny of anyone whose "name was not found written in the book of life" (v. 15). Although in the beginning there was only good, after responsible creatures (whether angelic or human) abused their freedom of choice to rebel against God, in the future there must always be both good and evil, heaven and hell. The only other options would be for God to remove freedom of choice or to annihilate the wicked, and these alternatives are contrary to the concept of a moral universe.

The Eternal Destiny of Believers
21:1 to 22:5

New Heaven and New Earth (21:1)

Basically, the Bible begins in a garden and ends in a garden. Yet between the two gardens a great deal of action, both sacred and secular, takes place. The sacred mainly concerns God's redemptive efforts, and the secular concerns mankind's sin, rebellion, and puny self-efforts to realize their true destiny. The overall story is about paradise lost and paradise regained. Because people sinned, the material world somehow suffered from mankind's fall (Gen. 3:17-18) and also will share in his redemption (Rom. 8:22-23). Although the prophet Isaiah was probably the first to envision an ideal society in which people "shall beat their swords into plowshares, and their spears into pruning hooks" (Isa. 2:4), others at different times also have dreamed of a perfect society. In his *Republic*, Plato conceived the idea of an ideal city-state. Much later Thomas More wrote his idealistic *Utopia*, (meaning "no place"), an imaginary island where perfect law, government, and peace prevailed. Roger Bacon wrote the *New Atlantis*, and Karl Marx wrote his *Communist Manifesto*, depicting a classless society. More recently, Franklin Roosevelt proposed his New Deal, Harry Truman his Square Deal, John F. Kennedy his New Frontier, and Lyndon B. Johnson his New Society.

The biblical term for the ideal society is the kingdom of God. Premillennialists envision the kingdom of God as realized on earth during Christ's literal reign of one thousand years, and later consummated in heaven. Amillennialists view the kingdom of God as an altogether spiritual reign, with the golden age of a perfect society being realized only in heaven. Postmillennialists believe in a thousand-year golden era, followed by Christ's return, which will usher in eternity.

Following Isaiah's lead (65:17), John wrote: "Then I saw a new heaven and a new earth; for the first heaven and the first earth had passed away, and the sea was no more" (v. 1). Peter also wrote of "new heavens and a new earth in which righteousness dwells" (2 Pet. 3:13). Heaven as well as earth will enjoy the newness that accompanies each believer's full redemption, including a new body to match the new life which began when the believer trusted Christ as Savior and Lord (2 Cor. 5:17).

In the new creation, there will be no "sea." As noted earlier, the sea represented danger, turmoil, restless masses of people, and separation. The first beast came up out of the sea (13:1). John saw a sea before God's throne (4:6), symbolizing his moral transcendence or holiness. On the Isle of Patmos, the sea separated John from those he dearly loved. Now in heaven there is no more sea, thus no more separation. Believers will enjoy God's presence in the fullest sense and have sweet fellowship around his throne. Since the redeemed will be saved even from the presence of sin, there will be no residue of sin to prevent them from enjoying intimate fellowship with God. Revelation seems to depict mankind's perfect environment as fulfilled in heaven, not during the millennium.

The New Jerusalem (21:2 to 22:5)

God's Presence and Comfort (21:2-4)

Although John earlier had introduced the subject of the marriage supper of the Lamb (19:9), we now see its fulfillment. In contrast to the worldly city, John "saw the holy city, new Jerusalem, coming down out of heaven from God, prepared as a bride adorned for her husband" (v. 2). Since a city consists primarily of people, not buildings, we note further that John "heard a great voice from the throne saying, 'Behold, the dwelling of God is with men. He will dwell with them, and they shall be his people, and God himself will be with them'" (v. 3). The word translated "dwelling" is the usual word for "tabernacle," and the verb for "will dwell" means "will tabernacle" or "will pitch tent." In fact, it is the identical verb used in John 1:14, which reads, "And the Word became flesh and dwelt among us." The tabernacle symbolized the presence of God. Thus, God became present with people in the person of Jesus Christ, who truly was Emmanuel, "God with us" (Matt. 1:23). Now God's tabernacle or presence will continue permanently with his children in a much fuller sense than they realized his presence during their earthly experience. As Paul wrote, "to depart and be with Christ . . . is far better" (Phil. 1:23). Although believers are God's people at all times, they will be his people in a more intimate and personal way in the new creation. While Moses in his human, finite state could see only the "back" of God (Ex. 33:23), in heaven all of God's people will see him face to face (1 Cor. 13:12). Even though now "we walk by faith, not by sight" (2 Cor. 5:7), then "we shall see him as he is" (1 John 3:2).

Verse 4 describes God's tender care for his children. "He will wipe away every tear from their eyes, and death shall be no more, neither shall there be mourning nor crying nor pain any more, for the former things have passed away." Some have wondered if tears may include those resulting from regret for deeds left undone, plus wasted opportunities to witness for Christ or minister to people in need. Apparently at some point God mercifully will blot out our remembrance of past failures and sins. Here the picture is one of perfect bliss. Death, mankind's greatest enemy, will no longer exist for believers. Moreover, the mourning, crying, and pain that accompany death will be unknown in the heavenly state. Although John probably meant "former things" in a bad sense, the expression may be broad enough to cover all earthly experiences and relationships. Despite our sentimental attachment to family and friends, will the heavenly state include reunion of earthly families? Jesus said to the Sadducees, "For in the resurrection they neither marry nor are given in marriage, but are like angels in heaven" (Matt. 22:30). When told that his mother and brothers wished to speak to him, Jesus replied, "For whoever does the will of my Father in heaven is my brother, sister, and mother" (Matt. 12:50). Although we apparently will recognize earthly family and friends in heaven, more importantly, all believers will make up one big, happy family of God. Moreover, our primary interest will be in praising him.

Consummation and Renewal (21:5-8)

God, of course, is the one "who sat upon the throne" and who said, "Behold, I make all things new" (v. 5a). Again the word for "new" means renewed, refreshed, or renovated, not the word that means altogether new. The statement "for these words are trustworthy and true" is God's most emphatic assurance to John that the vision of the new heaven and earth will certainly come to pass and that God himself will accomplish his purpose (v. 5b). The verb translated "It is done!" is plural and literally means "They have come to pass," perhaps indicating the accomplished renewal of both heaven and earth (v. 6a). Although yet future, the consummation of all things is just as certain as God's promise. Further assurance comes from the declaration, "I am the Alpha and the Omega, the beginning and the end" (v. 6a; 1:8; 22:13).

God additionally declared, "To the thirsty I will give from the fountain of the water of life without payment" (v. 6b; see 22:17). Since water is necessary for the life of human beings, animals, and plants, it became a common symbol for life. The psalmist compared the righteous person with "a tree planted by streams of water" (Ps. 1:3). Jesus said, "If any one thirst let him come to me and drink," and he went on to say, "Out of his heart shall flow rivers of living water" (John 7:37-38). Centuries earlier, Isaiah had uttered a similar invitation to "every one who thirsts" (55:1). "Without payment" means that eternal life is a gift of God, thus all of grace. "He who conquers" is the one who has faith in Christ and consequently "shall have his heritage" and enjoy a filial relationship with his Heavenly Father (v. 7).

In contrast to God's children, "as for the cowardly, the faithless, the polluted, as for murderers, fornicators, sorcerers, idolators, and all liars, their lot shall be in the lake that burns with fire and sulphur, which is the second death" (v. 8). Mention of the "cowardly" may relate particularly to those who did not have the courage to confess Jesus as Lord (Matt. 10:32-33). After Paul had given a similar list of sinners, who would not "inherit the kingdom of God," he added, "And such were some of you. But you were washed, you were sanctified, you were justified in the name of the Lord Jesus Christ and in the Spirit of our God" (1 Cor. 6:9,11). Consequently, forgiven sinners, whatever the nature of their sins, are no longer what they once were. They are truly God's children.

Description of the New Jerusalem (21:9-21)

According to verse 9, "one of the seven angels who had the seven bowls full of the seven last plagues" invited John to see "the Bride, the wife of the Lamb." However, the Bride turned out to be "the holy city Jerusalem coming down out of heaven from God" (v. 10b). John saw the holy city while "in the Spirit," after the angel had carried him to a "great, high mountain," (v. 10a), perhaps to be contrasted with the wilderness from which he had seen the harlot (17:3). Ezekiel recorded an experience very similar to that of John (40:2).

Verse 11 describes the New Jerusalem (the church) as "having the glory of God, its radiance like a most rare jewel, like a jasper, clear as crystal." Just as God's glory rubbed off on Moses and caused him to glow, it now has rubbed off on all of God's people. Paul wrote of "being changed into his likeness from one degree of glory to another" (2 Cor. 3:18). The holy city "had a great, high wall, with twelve gates, and at the gates twelve angels, and on the gates the

names of the twelve tribes of the sons of Israel were inscribed" (v.
12). Since walls were for protection, no doubt such symbolism was
meant here. Gates served both for opportunity to enter when open
and for protection when closed. In verse 21, we learn that "the
twelve gates were twelve pearls," and in verse 14 we note that the
wall "had twelve foundations, and on them the twelve names of the
twelve apostles of the Lamb" (also see Eph. 2:20). Like the twenty-
four elders, obviously the twelve gates and the twelve foundations
together symbolize spiritual Israel, the totality of all believers, both
Jews and Gentiles. Jesus himself said, "And I have other sheep, that
are not of this fold; I must bring them also, and they will heed my
voice. So there shall be one flock, one shepherd" (John 10:16).

Just as John earlier had measured the temple with an ordinary
measuring rod (11:1), the angel measured the holy city with a "rod
of gold" (v. 15). In both instances, the measuring apparently was
symbolic of divine protection and preservation. As we see in verse
16, the city was a perfect cube, measuring "twelve thousand stadia"
(1,500 miles) each direction. Those who compute the cubic feet of
space and then divide the total by the approximate amount of space
for one person to live comfortably, in order to arrive at the total
population, waste their time and effort. Since the holy of holies in
the tabernacle, as well as the three subsequent Jewish Temples, was
a perfect cube, symbolizing divine perfection, no doubt the same
symbolism applies here. John probably referred to the height of the
wall when he wrote that it measured "a hundred and forty-four
cubits by a man's measure, that is, an angel's" (v. 17). John's
somewhat vague reference to "an angel's" seems to mean that an
angel's measure is about the same as a man's. A cubit is the length
from the elbow to the end of the middle finger of an average man,
thus approximately eighteen inches. In comparison with the height
of the city, the wall was only some 216 feet high, yet still high
enough for protection and low enough for maximum visibility of the
beautiful city.

The majestic description in verses 18-21 depicts beauty, the like
of which defies the imagination. The precious stones are reminiscent of those on the breastplate of the high priest and serve as a
constant reminder that believers comprise a kingdom of priests
(1:6). Those who insist on a literal interpretation, and anticipate
walking down golden streets, seem largely to miss the spiritual

impact of this splendid sight. Absolute perfection is what John has described for us here. Although we make jokes about Saint Peter and the pearly gates, we seriously should realize that John used the most beautiful, most precious material substances on earth to describe a spiritual reality.

God's Glorious Presence (21:22-27)

Earlier John had indicated the presence of a temple in heaven (3:12; 7:15). God instructed Moses to make the tabernacle and its furniture according to the heavenly pattern (Ex. 25:9). The author of Hebrews argued that Christ's sacrifice was superior to that of the levitical priests because he went into the heavenly sanctuary (tabernacle), of which the earthly was a mere copy of type (Heb. 9:23-24). Why then did John write that he "saw no temple in the city, for its temple is the Lord God the Almighty and the Lamb" (v. 22)? What happened to the heavenly temple or tabernacle? In the first place, there was never a literal temple or tabernacle in heaven. Both are mere symbols of the presence of God. Now, in the full presence of God, there is no need for a symbol. In fact, the heavenly city, a perfect cube, was not only a temple; it was the innermost sanctuary, the holy of holies, which symbolized God's presence more than did the temple (tabernacle) as a whole.

Furthermore, "the city has no need of sun or moon to shine upon it, for the glory of God is its light, and its lamp is the Lamb" (v. 23). Throughout the Bible, light is a symbol of God and also of holiness and righteousness. On the other hand, darkness is a symbol of sin and unrighteousness. Jesus said, "For every one who does evil hates the light, and does not come to the light, lest his deeds should be exposed. But he who does what is true comes to the light, that it may be clearly seen that his deeds have been wrought in God" (John 3:20-21). Just as both God and the Lamb are the temple of heaven, they also are the light. Although "glory" has several shades of meaning, here it refers to God's lustrous majesty and magnificence.

According to verse 24, "By its light shall the nations walk; and the kings of the earth shall bring their glory into it." This passage closely resembles Isaiah 60:3,11. The emphasis seems to be on the fact that people from all nations will be included among the saints who occupy, and in a sense *are*, the holy city. Earlier John had described the innumerable multitude "from every nation, from all tribes and peoples and tongues" (7:9). We need to keep in mind that John intended to describe a spiritual reality, not a literal city and its occupants. The fact that "its gates shall never be shut by day—and there shall be no night there" is evidence of security, openness, opportunity for going in and out (also see John 10:9), and lack of fear from evil done under the cover of darkness (v. 25).

Like verse 24, verse 26 reflects the teaching of Isaiah 60:3,11, which may have a dual meaning: (1) the restoration of Israel to a place of prominence and blessing following the Babylonian Exile and (2) a foreshadowing of the consummation of spiritual Israel, consisting of God's redeemed from both national Israel and the Gentiles. Because of this duality and overlap, we must be careful not to confuse the material aspect with the spiritual. Regardless of the exact meaning of the symbolism, we are wrong to think of heaven in materialistic terms. Jesus never tried to win disciples by promising them that their sacrifices on earth would pale into insignificance when compared with the materialistic splendor and wealth of heaven. Unfortunately, the "many mansions" phrase of the King James Version (John 14:2) has led some people to believe that one day every Christian will live in a house that is more spacious, comfortable, and lavish than the White House. The actual translation is "many rooms," meaning that there is room enough in God's house for everyone. Thus, verse 26 means that all "the glory and the honor of the nations" will now be attributed to the heavenly city because all of God's children are kings and priests.

Perhaps still contrasting the harlot (Rome) with the heavenly city, John wrote, "But nothing unclean shall enter it, nor any one who practices abomination or falsehood" (v. 27a). For "unclean" John used a word meaning common, here denoting profane or vulgar. Although the same word was used to designate ceremonially unclean food and people (Rom. 14:14), John particularly meant immoral people. The word for "abomination" describes anything that is detestable to God and therefore arouses his wrath since his nature is eternally opposed to evil. As shown elsewhere in John's writings (John 8:44; 1 John 2:21,27), a "falsehood" (lie) is altogether contrary to God's nature and thus repugnant to God. The qualification "but only those who are written in the Lamb's book of life" (v. 27b) rules out the possibility that John meant unregenerate nations in verse 24 unless, of course, we reject the concept of the eternal separation of the just from the unjust (20:15; Matt. 25:46; Luke 16:26).

Eternal Life Depicted (22:1-5)

The heavenly city would not be complete without "the river of the water of life," which John described as "bright as crystal, flowing from the throne of God and of the Lamb through the middle of the street of the city (vv. 1-2a). This description reminds us of the Garden of Eden through which a "river flowed" and then "divided and became four rivers" (Gen. 2:10). To somewhat nomadic people, who often experienced a scarcity of water, the Israelites used water as a symbol of life. Previously we noted how Jesus used water as a symbol of eternal life. During the Exodus travels, God provided water from a mysterious rock that seemed to follow the Israelites. Moses' great sin involved striking the rock instead of speaking to it (Num. 20:10-13). Later Paul wrote, "For they drank from the supernatural Rock which followed them, and the Rock was Christ" (1 Cor. 10:4). Naturally Paul used symbolism just as John did here.

The heavenly scene is both spectacular and beautiful. Instead of a sea before God's throne (4:6), now there is a river flowing from it right through the middle of heaven's main street. "Also, on either side of the river [is] the tree of life with its twelve kinds of fruit, yielding its fruit each month; and the leaves of the tree were for the healing of the nations" (v. 2b). John apparently derived this scene in part from Ezekiel's depiction of the temple with a river flowing from it (47:1), with the added description: "And on the banks, on both sides of the river, there will grow all kinds of trees for food. Their leaves will not wither nor their fruit fail, but they will bear fresh fruit every month, because the water for them flows from the sanctuary. Their fruit will be for food, and their leaves for healing" (47:12). Whereas the old Eden had both the "tree of life" and the "tree of the knowledge of good and evil" (Gen. 2:9), the new Eden has only the "tree of life." Since the number twelve is symbolic of religion or spiritual things, the "twelve kinds of fruit, yielding its fruit each month" must refer to spiritual food. Moreover, the "healing of the nations" also must be symbolic of the ongoing spiritual health of those from all nations who make up the family of God. The tree of life in both the original garden and the new garden is the same tree. The tree represents eternal life.

According to the Old Testament, every person and thing were

dedicated to God either for blessing or cursing, either for mercy or judgment, for salvation or damnation, for preservation or destruction (not annihilation). The Hebrew term *cherem* as well as its Greek equivalent, *anathema*, refers to someone or something dedicated to God for destruction. Because of the principle of *solidarity*, when Achan took some loot from Jericho, which had been put under the *cherem* (ban), he put himself and his family under the *cherem*, resulting in utter destruction of himself and all he possessed (Josh. 7:10-26). Later the principle of *individual responsibility* prevailed as Ezekiel wrote, "The soul that sins shall die. The son shall not suffer for the iniquity of the father, nor the father suffer for the iniquity of the son; the righteousness of the righteous shall be upon himself, and the wickedness of the wicked shall be upon himself" (18:20). The Mosaic law pronounced a curse on all who did not keep it (Deut. 27:26). It also pronounced a curse upon anyone hanged upon a tree (Deut. 21:23). According to Paul, Jesus took the latter curse upon himself in order to redeem those (all people) under the first curse (Gal. 3:13). Thus, in the fullest sense, John could write, "There shall no more be anything accursed" in the holy city (v. 3*a*). Although Jesus *potentially* saved all by his redemptive sacrifice, only those who repent of their sins and commit their lives to him as Savior and Lord are *actually* saved. Therefore, all who reject him will not share in the new Jerusalem and thus will remain "accursed" and separated from it.

"But the throne of God and of the Lamb shall be in it, and his servants shall worship him" (v. 3*b*). This statement stresses the centrality of the Heavenly Father and Son and suggests that worship will be the main activity in the heavenly city. We observed earlier that the most faithful of God's servants on earth could not see God in his fullness. As John wrote in his Gospel, "No one has ever seen God" (1:18). Now John could write, "they shall see his face, and his name shall be on their foreheads" (v. 4). This passage assures intimate fellowship eternally, with complete security, for those who are God's very own people. Verse 5 reiterates the truth expressed in 21:25 concerning the absence of night, which symbolizes sin and danger. Additionally, verse 5 repeats the truth of 21:23 that "they need no light of lamp or sun, for the Lord God will be their light." Somewhat like adding the icing to a cake, John completed his description of the heavenly scene by asserting, "and they shall reign for ever and ever." John perhaps intended a contrast between eternity and the saints' millennial reign with Christ, which was relatively long. Yet, compared with their eternal reign, the millennium, whether interpreted literally or figuratively, was brief. For example, Peter wrote "that with the Lord one day is a thousand years, and a thousand years as one day" (2 Pet. 3:8). Although this writer has tried to be fair to other views, he has concluded that the millennium is symbolic of the period of time between the first and second advents of Christ. Therefore, the saints' ruling with Christ both during the millennium and throughout eternity is a spiritual reign.

Epilogue
22:6-21

The angel said to John, "These words are trustworthy and true" (v. 6a), repeating God's words of affirmation concerning his making all things new (21:5). The angel further stressed the truthfulness of the disclosures to John by adding, "And the Lord, the God of the spirits of the prophets, has sent his angel to show his servants what must soon take place" (v. 6b). Earlier the angel had said, "For the testimony of Jesus is the spirit of prophecy" (19:10). The angel's statement here seems to affirm two truths: (1) The same God who spoke through the Old Testament prophets has spoken through the message given to John; (2) God sent his angel to disclose to "his servants" (John and fellow believers) the events soon to occur.

Although the Revised Standard Version includes the statement, "And behold, I am coming soon" (v. 7a), as part of the angel's message, it appears to be a statement by the glorified Christ (2:16; 3:11). Since God does not reckon time as we do, "soon" does not necessarily mean immediately. However, it implies a call to readiness and expectancy.

The sixth Beatitude appears in the promise, "Blessed is he who keeps the words of the prophecy of this book" (v. 7b). Although we cannot tell whether this Beatitude came from Christ, the angel, or John, the truth is the same. The verb "keeps" includes heeding the message set forth in Revelation, which, among other things, is a "prophecy." Although prophecy involves much more than prediction, there is a great deal of prediction in Revelation. As noted heretofore, the Revelation's overall message is clear, but because of the abundance of symbolic language, we cannot be absolutely certain about the details.

In verse 8, John emphasized the fact that he personally "heard and saw these things." Even though his reputation as God's servant was at stake, John gladly attested to the authenticity of both the message he heard and the visions he saw. John seemingly "fell down to worship at the feet of the angel" twice (v. 8; 19:10). However, the statement here may be a reminder to his readers of his earlier action, since his conclusion in part repeats matters already mentioned. Unless John was unusually excited, and thus not thinking clearly, we find his making the same serious mistake twice unlikely. In either case, the angel's response is essentially the same: "You must not do that! I am a fellow servant with you and your brethren the prophets, and with those who keep the words of this book. Worship God" (v. 8b). You may wish to review the comments on 19:10 concerning the problem of angel worship. Only God the Creator, never the creature, is worthy of worship.

Although John was told to seal up the words uttered by the seven thunders (10:4), now the instructions are: "Do not seal up the words of the prophecy of this book, for the time is near" (v. 10). The prophetic message of Revelation was to be shared, not only with the seven churches of Asia, but with Christians everywhere. While John and others who wrote about Christ's return spoke as if it might occur in their own lifetimes, they never specified an exact date. Regardless of when he may return, we should always live expectantly.

The remainder of the angel's message offends some people because they misinterpret it: "Let the evildoer still do evil, and the filthy still be filthy, and the righteous still do right, and the holy still be holy" (v. 11). These instructions do not represent fatalistic resignation to conditions as they are. Rather, they indicate a realistic view of human society. In Jesus' parable of the tares in the field, the landlord said to his servants, "Let both grow together until the harvest" (Matt. 13:30). Similarly, Paul contrasted believers with unbelievers when he wrote, "So then let us not sleep, as others do, but let us keep awake and be sober. For those who sleep sleep at night, and those who get drunk are drunk at night" (1 Thess. 5:6-7). People make their own choices for good or evil.

Verses 12-13 represent the words of Christ: "Behold, I am coming soon, bringing my recompense, to repay every one for what he has done. I am the Alpha and the Omega, the first and the last, the beginning and the end." The same words, earlier applied to the Father (1:8; 21:6), apply fully to the Son. Since the word translated "recompense" is used elsewhere concerning the righteous and the unrighteous, probably it includes both in the present context. Again we note the principle of judgment according to works, which are a sure clue to one's character.

Verse 14 contains the seventh and final Beatitude in Revelation. Those are "Blessed" (happy) "who wash their robes, that they may have the right to the tree of life and that they may enter the city by the gates." Some Greek manuscripts read "they that do his commandments" instead of "who wash their robes," but the difference in meaning is not great. The figure of washing their robes is equivalent to trusting Christ concerning his sacrificial death on their behalf. In the final analysis, the real entrance to the heavenly city is through him who said, "I am the door; if any one enters by me, he will be saved" (John 10:9). Those "Outside" the gates did not wash their robes and are characterized as "dogs and sorcerers and fornicators and murderers and idolators, and every one who loves and practices falsehood" (v. 15; 21:8). The term "dogs" was a label of reproach and baseness. The Jews commonly used it to refer to Gentiles, and the Old Testament once uses the term *dog* to designate a sodomite or male prostitute (Deut. 23:18). For discussion of the other terms, refer to the comments on 21:8.

According to verse 16, the risen, glorified Lord said, "I Jesus have sent my angel to you with this testimony for the churches. I am the root and the offspring of David, the bright morning star." Thus, Christ himself authenticated the message contained in the Book of Revelation. As the Jewish Messiah, Jesus was a descendant of David, even though he refused the messianic role of popular expectation (John 6:15). As "the bright morning star" (see 2:28), he is the dawning of eternal day for all who place their trust in him.

Appropriately, Revelation includes an invitation to eternal life for all who have not yet partaken of it: "The Spirit and the Bride say, 'Come.' And let him who hears say, 'Come.' And let him who is thirsty come, let him who desires take the water of life without price" (v. 17). Although some relate this invitation to Christ's own coming, the central thought concerns a final appeal to all unrepentant sinners to turn from their sins to Christ. Sinners still have time to partake of the living water. The expression "without price" means that salvation is totally a gift of divine grace (Isa. 55:1). The "Spirit" refers to the Holy Spirit, and the "Bride" refers, of course, to the church, the total body of believers on earth. The expression, "let him who hears," implies that recipients of the gospel are to share it with others (Rom. 1:14).

When the Israelites arrived in Canaan and assembled between Mount Gerizim (blessing) and Mount Ebal (cursing), a choirlike group on Mount Gerizim pronounced God's blessings upon an obedient people and his curses upon a disobedient people (Deut. 11:26-29). John, like other ancient writers (Deut. 4:2; Prov. 30:6; 2 Pet. 3:16), pronounced a blessing upon those who heeded his words (v. 7) and a curse on anyone who tampered with them (v. 18). John's warning is so severe that it includes suffering "the plagues described in this book" for anyone who adds to his words, and deprivation of one's share "in the tree of life and in the holy city" for anyone who "takes away from the words of the book of this prophecy." Despite the severity of John's warning, we must urge caution on two matters. First, we should not use this passage as a proof text to support the doctrine of falling from grace or losing one's salvation. Second, we should not use this passage as a club against those who disagree with our own interpretation of Revelation. On the other hand, we always need to be prayerfully and reverently careful about our interpretation of any portion of God's Word. When James wrote that "we who teach shall be judged with greater strictness" (3:1), he reiterated the principle that greater opportunity always entails greater responsibility (Matt. 11:20-24).

Verse 20 is further authentication that Christ himself is the real author and authority of Revelation's message. The words, "Surely I am coming soon," represent a solemn promise, and the seeming delay does not mean that scoffers are right when they say, "Where is the promise of his coming?" (2 Pet. 3:3-4). Rather, the seeming delay may represent God's mercy and a further opportunity for repentance (2 Pet. 3:9). After all, time in contrast to eternity is like the batting of an eye and thus extremely relative. The words,

"Amen. Come, Lord Jesus!" reflect John's personal hope. In Aramaic, the native Jewish dialect, "Come, Lord Jesus!" is *maranatha* and constitutes a very early Christian prayer (1 Cor. 16:22). Then as a fitting benediction, John concluded his triumphant and hope-inspiring message with the words, "The grace of the Lord Jesus be with all the saints. Amen." (v. 21).

As a sort of review and summary of Revelation, I wish to point up several important matters. First, despite the problem of symbolism, the overall message is abundantly clear. Christ and the forces of righteousness eventually will triumph completely over Satan and the forces of evil. Although the final victory has not been won historically, from the divine viewpoint the victory is already an accomplished fact. Second, regardless of our own inclinations about the consummation of history, we violate the principles of sound biblical interpretation if we ignore the historical context in which Revelation was written. Thus, the first question we must ask is: What did the Book of Revelation mean to its original readers? If it did not make sense to them, we are very presumptuous to assume that we can understand it better than they did. Another principle of biblical interpretation is highly important. Every passage of Scripture has one central meaning as intended by the writer. Although it may have many applications, it has only one basic meaning. Although a person must choose one of the various approaches to Revelation, not a single one is completely free of error. Consequently, we need to be open to God and the leadership of the Holy Spirit as we study the Book of Revelation. At the same time, we must be wary of anyone who claims that his own interpretation exclusively has the Holy Spirit's stamp of approval.

The approach of this commentary has been to interpret Revelation, a prophetic book, in light of Old Testament prophecy, which often has both an immediate application and an extended application, perhaps what may be called a double intent. Therefore, this writer has concluded that Revelation primarily relates to the problem of first-century Roman persecution of the church. Yet Revelation's message spills over into the future and thus still has a coming fulfillment. Although the future entered the present when God became incarnate in the person of Jesus Christ, the future is yet awaiting final fulfillment. While the kingdom of God is now present, it still awaits its consummation at the second coming of

Christ. Contrary to the view that history endlessly repeats itself, the biblical revelation discloses that history had a specific beginning and that it will have a definite end. Moreover, despite our inability to understand fully God's handiwork in history, the Book of Revelation affirms God's sovereignty over history through which he is working out his grand purpose of redemption. As Paul so fittingly wrote, "For now we see in a mirror dimly, but then face to face. Now I know in part; then I shall understand fully, even as I have been fully understood" (1 Cor. 13:12).

Notes

1. Ray Frank Robbins, *The Revelation of Jesus Christ* (Nashville: Broadman Press, 1975), p. 225.

2. George R. Beasley-Murray, Herschel H. Hobbs, Ray F. Robbins, David C. George, *Revelation: Three Viewpoints* (Nashville: Broadman Press, 1977), p. 62.

Bibliography

Arndt, William F., and F. Wilbur Gingrich. *A Greek-English Lexicon of the New Testament and Other Early Christian Literature.* Chicago: The University of Chicago Press, 1957.

Ashcraft, Morris. *Revelation* in *The Broadman Bible Commentary,* Vol. 12. Nashville: Broadman Press, 1972.

Barclay, William. *The Letters of John and Jude* in *The Daily Study Bible.* Philadelphia: The Westminster Press, 1960.

Barclay, William. *The Revelation of John,* 2 vols., in *The Daily Study Bible.* Philadelphia: The Westminster Press, 1960.

Barnett, Albert E. *The Epistle of Jude* (Introduction and Exegesis) in *The Interpreter's Bible,* Vol. 12. New York: Abingdon Press, 1957.

Beasley-Murray, G. R., Herschel H. Hobbs, and Ray Frank Robbins, with summary by David C. George. *Revelation: Three Viewpoints.* Nashville: Broadman Press, 1977.

Bowman, John Wick. *The Drama of the Book of Revelation.* Philadelphia: The Westminster Press, 1945.

Caird, G. B. *A Commentary on the Revelation of St. John the Divine.* New York: Harper & Row, Publishers, 1966.

De Haan, M. R. *Revelation.* Grand Rapids: Zondervan Publishing House, 1946.

Ellul, Jacques. *Apocalypse: The Book of Revelation.* New York: The Seabury Press, 1977.

Erdman, Charles R. *The General Epistles.* Philadelphia: The Westminster Press, 1919.

Ezell, Douglas. *Revelations on Revelation.* Waco: Word Books, 1977.

Hendriksen, W. *More Than Conquerors.* Grand Rapids: Baker Book House, 1959.

Houlden, J. L. *A Commentary on the Johannine Epistles* in *Harper's New Testament Commentaries.* New York: Harper & Row, Publishers, 1973.

Kiddle, Martin. *The Revelation of St. John* in *The Moffatt New Testament Commentary.* New York: Harper and Brothers Publishers [n.d.].

Kuyper, Abraham. *The Revelation of St. John.* Grand Rapids: William B. Eerdmans Publishing Company, 1963.

Ladd, George Eldon. *A Commentary on the Revelation of John.* Grand Rapids: William B. Eerdmans Publishing Company, 1972.

Lenski, R. C. H. *The Interpretation of St. John's Revelation.* Columbus: The Wartburg Press, 1943.

Love, Julian Price. *The First, Second, and Third Letter of John; The Letter of Jude; The Revelation to John* in *The Layman's Bible Commentary,* vol. 25. Richmond: John Knox Press, 1960.

Mauro, Philip. *Of Things Which Soon Must Come to Pass.* Grand Rapids: Wm. B. Eerdmans Publishing Co., 1933.

McDowell, Edward A. *1,2,3 John* in *The Broadman Bible Commentary,* Vol. 12. Nashville: Broadman Press, 1972.

McDowell, Edward A. *The Meaning and Message of the Book of Revelation.* Nashville: Broadman Press, 1951.

Moody, Dale. *The Letters of John.* Waco: Word Books, Publishers, 1970.

Pieters, Albertus. *Studies in The Revelation of St. John.* Grand Rapids: Wm. B. Eerdmans Publishing Company, 1943.

Ramsay, W. M. *The Letters to the Seven Churches of Asia.* Grand Rapids: Baker Book House, 1963.

Rist, Martin. *The Revelation of St. John the Divine* (Introduction and Exegesis) in *The Interpreter's Bible,* Vol. 12. New York: Abingdon Press, 1957.

Robbins, Ray Frank. *The Revelation of Jesus Christ.* Nashville: Broadman Press, 1975.

Ross, Alexander. *Commentary on the Epistles of James and John.* Grand Rapids: Wm. B. Eerdmans Publishing Company, 1954.

Seiss, J. A. *The Apocalypse.* Philadelphia: Philadelphia School of the Bible, 1865.

Stott, J. R. W. *Commentary on the Johannine Epistles* in *The Tyndale New Testament Commentaries.* Grand Rapids: Wm. B. Eerdmans Publishing Company, 1964.

Summers, Ray. *Jude* in *The Broadman Bible Commentary,* Vol. 12. Nashville: Broadman Press, 1972.

Summers, Ray. *Worthy Is the Lamb.* Nashville: Broadman Press, 1951.

Swete, Henry Barclay. *Commentary on the Apocalypse of St. John.* Grand Rapids: Wm. B. Eerdmans Publishing Company, 1951.

Tenney, Merrill C. *Interpretating Revelation.* Grand Rapids: Wm. B. Eerdmans Publishing Company, 1957.

Wilder, Amos N. *The First, Second, and Third Epistles of John* (Introduction and Exegesis) in *The Interpreter's Bible,* Vol. 12. New York: Abingdon Press, 1957.